I-Conomics

The Economics of Personal Influence

This book is dedicated to all those who started with a dream and fulfilled those dreams through perseverance and determination. In life we learn that leadership is not following the path others have defined, nor always agreeing with the status quo, but to seek truth in a world of quick answers and chatty opinions. Leadership is the beckoning call of the compass that flawlessly faces north even when each road starts the same. It is to set on the mantle of time one tick of the clock in a series of ticks. Most of all leadership is enlightenment for the next generation even when such knowledge comes at a heavy price.

Table of Contents

Path-Goal Theory

Finding a Path to Higher Organizational Performance

"Many are stubborn in pursuit of the path they have chosen,

few in pursuit of the goal." -Friedrich Nietzsche

Leadership Paths to Organizational Achievement

Path-Goal Theory

Organizations are complex beasts that have an abundance of working components moving in varying directions at any given time that impact the strategic success of the company. Executives often find themselves at a loss when trying to implement strategies that on the surface appear sound but ultimately fail to produce meaningful results. Planners may not have taken into consideration the needs of employees, how these employees determine which tasks they will complete, and how this influences the productivity of the organization. It is often these subtle and difficult to define concepts that make or break successful policy implementation. Path-goal theory works with employees expectancies to help executives understand how their behavior, the structure of the organizations, the methods of rewards, and employee needs all come together to create collective productivity.

Path-goal theory creates a method to overcome business obstacles and problems by matching appropriate goals to employee needs. They can be applied on an organizational level or on an individual level but primarily is designed for unit level improvement. As individuals are fundamental building blocks of the organizational strategy, their needs should not be ignored in the strategic planning process. Path-goal theory helps explain complex organizational behavior in order to adjust that behavior to a more productive end. By understanding the satisfaction, motivation and performance of subordinates, leaders can find new ways of meeting market challenges. These challenges are met by encouraging all partners to take paths that maximize the collective strategic opportunities of the organization.

Executive Actions and Employee Performance

One of the first tasks new executives complete once hired is the creation of a strategy on how to enhance those areas under their influence. Unfortunately, the majority of strategies fail because they have not developed either the internal structure (pathways) or the employees attributes (contingencies) to fulfill these goals. In like instances, the structure does not allow for the maximum organizational performance level due to a number of unseen internal constraints. Path-goal theory helps organizational leaders understand the nuances of achieving goals by understanding the multiple factors that influences its potential for success or failure. Ignoring any aspect of the system's development ultimately means failure and financial loss when the pieces don't come together just right.

Leader's ultimate responsibilities rely upon managing a larger system to produce positive financial outcomes. When they cannot, their leadership is deemed a failure. Those leaders who can provide and develop appropriate structure are rated higher and have more productive workgroups (Filley & House, 1969). Therefore, leadership behavior should be seen in a context of organizational structure and the encouraging of clear pathways where employee attributes are maximized. Behavior outside of this perspective is likely to either confuse or mislead employees while creating havoc on growth potential.

Path-goal theory helps understand unit performance based on 1.) the leader's behaviors and 2.) situational contingencies that modify those behaviors (Barling, et. al., 2011). Leadership behaviors are influenced by a number of environmental factors. These environmental factors are often limited by the constraints within the organization and the pressures that factor into the leader's choices. Pressure may take the form of political, social, or financial aspects and naturally influences both choices and behaviors which in turn impacts employee performance.

House (1996) describes the two main concepts associated with path-goal theory as 1.) followers will see leaders behaviors as valid if that behavior leads to their satisfaction or future satisfaction and, 2.) such behavior is considered successful if it provides paths to that satisfaction as contingent on their performance. Employees follow those who help them succeed and define such pathways that lead to goal achievement. When personal leadership styles build trust and offer appropriate paths of goal attainment such leaders are seen as more worthy than those who cannot communicate appropriately and follow up on their statements.

Employees naturally look to their leaders to cue their own actions and behaviors. The actions and words of a leader create an impression on followers and guide them to understanding how rewards and efforts are connected. The more clearly they understand the process the more likely they are able to make decisions that lead to their own awards. The contingencies further define the congruence between leadership priming of behavior and the expected practical achievement of subordinate goals.

Robert House's original 1971 research study tried to determine the validity of three hypotheses:

1. Leadership induced structure improves path instrumentality by reducing ambiguity.

2. Leaders influence the subjective values groups assign to outcomes.

3. Leadership induced structure will have different impacts on whether or not subordinates see the tasks as positive or negative as well as clear or ambiguous.

He found the effects of leadership induced structure were differential, depending on the job autonomy and decision level of the employees. Higher skilled employees with more ambiguity in their jobs generally performed better when specific paths were developed that would define effort and rewards while less skilled employees whose jobs were already pre-defined resented leadership induced structures. With white collar workers induced structure clarified ambiguity but in blue collar workers it was considered a change in the *status quo*.

Change cannot be sought for change sake and without adequate explanation change will often be seen as an issue related to leadership power dynamics. When such changes are brought forward without appropriate explanation or vision they are more likely to be resented than those that seem to enhance goals of people. Leaders will need to ensure changes are beneficial, create greater alignment between paths and goals, and explained well to create appropriate context.

Furthermore, leaders often influenced the values employees assign to outcomes. This helps indicate that employees take their cues from their leaders to determine what rewards they should be seeking and how they can work to achieve them. In many ways, leaders have an important function of defining and developing the social and structural environment that leads to organizational performance. Communication is one aspect them helps them create influence and context for needed change and behavioral adjustments.

How and why such acceptance or rejection of induced changes occurred was based primarily in the perception of how employees viewed such adjustments. White collar workers who seek to produce meaningful results and obtain additional rewards often welcome clarification but lower skilled workers whose jobs and potential rewards are already pre-defined generally resented change. To encourage blue collar workers to accept such structure they should see it as an opportunity to meaningfully contribute to the organizational outcomes as well as a path to earn additional rewards.

Stimulant and Change

At a deeper level, the theory attempts to predict subordinate performance by understanding what they are thinking (expectancy) and what behavior they will display under certain situations (performance) based upon leadership behavior (priming). In other words, it is a correlation-based historical effect of leadership and subordinate behavior to make predictions about future behaviors (Mawhinney & Ford, 1977). When the multiple factors are understood, it is possible to see the most likely employee choices based upon the strategic pathways and understandings the employees have gained.

Under a variety of conditions, employees will respond in predictable ways which lends itself to the power of leading. There is a stimulant (a force) and a response (reactive force). By understanding which situational and behavioral stimulations elicit employee's performance the organization can work on creating the right structure, behavioral expectations, environment and rewards to produce the right effect. Since this is not a simple correlation, like someone instinctively moving their hand from a hot stove, the factors can become quite complex and therefore lead to a host of different conclusions.

The strength or weaknesses of the responses to stimulant behavior are based in need to obtain comfort (i.e. rewards) and avoid discomfort (i.e. punishment). This is often denoted as S+ (reinforcement) and S- (negative reinforcement). As reinforcement is provided, positive employee behaviors increase while if negative reinforcement occur the positive behavior decreases (Herrnstein, 1970). This process applies to humans as much as it does to animal species and is a fundamental experience of organizational homeostasis when forces and pressures are aligned.

In the workplace, an intermittent schedule of positive reinforcement or negative reinforcement comes from either the social environment or the financial network. Positive social reinforcement may come in terms of praise, acceptance, recognition, honors and awards. Negative reinforcements are most often experienced in the form of rejection, disapproval, criticism, or other social detractors while the financial network provides compensation in terms of raises, vacation time, seniority, or anything else of tangible value. The workers environment is the totality of these experiences.

According to Mawhinney & Ford (1976), behavior can be predicted based upon the strength or weakness of reinforcement. The behavior can be written into a formula $B1/B2=R1/R2$ whereby B1 and B2 are opposing behaviors which are reinforced by R1 and R2. The ratios equal each other and can predict behaviors in both animals and humans. He uses the examples of B1 as task behaviors and B0 being non-task behaviors. Likewise, R1 is all behaviors corresponding to task reinforcement while R0 corresponding to non-task reinforcement. They can be noted as:

Behavior: $B1 + B0 = K$

Behavior is a total result of task and non-task actions.

Reinforcements: $R1 + R0 = V$

Reinforcement schedule is a result of task and non-task reinforcement.

For example, an employee's spends 60% of their time in task related behavior and 40% of their time in non-task related behavior. We might say that the employee spends 60% of their time doing meaningful work and 40% of their time walking around the office socializing. If increases in positive reinforcement relate to an increase in task related performances the employee is likely to adjust their behavior to achieve their goals. If the employee experiences positive reinforcement after they have increased non-task related behaviors such non-task behavior will likely increase.

As certain task performance behaviors increase B1 there should be a corresponding increase in reinforcements R1 to further encourage the behavior in the future. These reinforcements could come in the form of social praise, promotions, recognition, income, job expansion or any number of other positive benefits. As behavior is exhibited and rewards reinforce such behavior, it will become more likely. The same can be said for non-task behavior and the possibility of rewards thereafter. It is possible to extinct behavior by limiting or offering rewards.

Over a particular time-span the positive and negative reinforces are mixed in an intermittent and sometimes random schedule throughout the environment. For example, managers could reward positive behavior with recognition from supervisors and at the same time provide a mixed message of disdain or jealousy. These mixed messages create confusion among employees and possibly impact future performance as these employees attempt to understand the non-verbal messages that are transmitted. The total environmental collection of these positive and negative reinforcement cues is what is important in determining the success of creating motivating pressure to encourage positive employee behavior.

Employees scan their environments and will decide to further engage or disengage depending on their impressions (i.e. positive and negative reinforcement). These impressions are often subjective but when dealing with a diverse population with different background experiences the subjectivity becomes more objective. This is one reason larger surveys are more accurate in determining how a company or other entity is functioning in terms of providing positive momentum to encourage performance.

Employees that are encouraged by their environments will often develop methods of achievement based upon present and past experience. The concept of similar responses in a variety of situations is called a stimulus generalization (Millenson, 1970). When situations appear similar to a past situation where certain behaviors elicited positive results, that behavior will likely be used again to accomplish goals. We use our experiences and present information to make assessments about which behavior we should exhibit to obtain future rewards; the predictive value.

Past performance is a fairly strong predictor of future performance. It is not a perfect predictor as people can discriminate different situational factors that may lead them to new conclusions and therefore new behaviors. The more complex a person's intellectual ability the more successful they are in finding both the similarities and discriminators to determine the best courses of action. They are not limited to simple automatic or previous learned responses even if the majority of the population is.

Leadership, Structure and Influence

Leadership behavior is not blindly accepted or mimicked by followers. Emulated behavior is situational and contextual. According to research by Kim, et. al. (2004) those behaviors will only be acceptable if they fit within the cultural context and values of the people being led. If such behaviors are outside of employees understandings, they will reject such leaders and their behavior. Leadership constraints help to ensure the leader is focused on the needs of the group versus having ulterior motives or unacceptable values.

The ultimate goal of human resources management should be to set upon a strategy and reduce any hindrances to employees seeking to obtain appropriate individual and collective goals. For example, if a company desires to develop additional sales revenue they should define their goals and make effort on the most appropriate paths. These goals could include sales quotas, productivity measures, quality improvements, cost measures, or anything else beneficial to the overall strategy. The values and leadership behavior must consistently support those goals in order for them to be effective.

Hindrance and roadblocks come in many different forms that range from management personality to organizational structure. Human resources professions are advocates and analysts that help develop better methods for operating the business. That growth should always be rooted in the development of employee's skills to meet the strategic objectives of the company. If there is an organizational roadblock to that higher performance changes need to be made to ensure effectiveness of employee effort.

The key benefit of path-goal theory is that it creates pathways that lead to higher levels of goal achievement. When employees pick appropriate paths, they should be rewarded to maintain their motivation and development. The theory is based off of Martin Evan's work (1970) which indicates that leadership effectiveness and employee's perceptions influence their choice in behaviors (path) that leads to appropriate outcomes (goal)(Evans, 1970).

This theory historically has a positive impact on company performance. As an example, Columbia Records inspired to improve performance, contentment, and motivation by clarifying paths on how to achieve goals, rewarding employees once they have achieved those defined goals, and removed organizational obstacles that lowered the chances of employees being successful (Vandergrift & Matusitz, 2011). This level of organizational obtainment could not occur unless the company decision makers are aware of the roadblocks to successful performance and set upon a strategy to reduce them.

The induced structure as provided in the policies, procedures, compensation measurements, performance appraisals, tools, social expectations, and the general environment add up to help clarify goals and expectations. If there is incongruence between the effort and reward the structure of the organization has a flaw which will limit its ability to succeed. As the leader is the general catalyst to this structure they take precedence within the theory.

Leadership Style

One of the first components to path-goal theory is the type of leadership enacted and its potential influence and impact on employee's behavior. As employees take cues and information from their leaders they can create higher levels of organizational performance through higher expectations. According to House and Mitchell (1974) there are four kinds of leadership behavior:

1. Directive path-goal clarifying leadership behavior: This behavior offers a structure and methodology to expected behavior. It includes allowing subordinates to know what their job entails, clarify expectations, and the type of rewards a person should receive.

2. Supportive leader behavior: This behavior encourages a psychological bond with employees by showing a level of concern over their needs. The goal is to reduce stress, create social networks and encourage performance.

3. Participative leader behavior: This behavior seeks to draw people into decision-making by encouraging participation and validating their ideas. This type of leadership can encourage others to take ownership over their actions and results.

4. Achievement oriented behavior: This behavior seeks to improve performance by setting goals and encouraging employee confidence. The leader provides defined goals, motivation, and feedback.

The type of leadership styles executives and individual members of the management team choose can have a large systematic influence on the functioning of the organization. Some exceptional leaders can show a level of the multiple forms leadership and can use these varying approaches to create successful organizations. This includes the ability to give clear directions when needed (transactional), show a level of concern over employees (supportive), draw employees into solutions (participative), and set clear goals (achievement). Most executives have a particular style that filters throughout their department and becomes a contributor to the organizational culture.

Leadership behavior is not static and changes based upon the situation. As employees assess their needs, the resources available, and the political environment their behavior will change in an effort to seek out the most likely paths. Eagly and Johnson (1990) describe such leadership behavior as a range of normal behaviors which are situational by nature. New situations should bring new leadership styles.

Situational behavior indicates that as the environment change so does the leader's behavior. For example, a leader who is managing a company that is going through bankruptcy will act in different ways than one that is at the head of a growing organization. Each situation requires a different style in order to overcome obstacles. This environment is defined by the totality of the leader's understanding and experiences.

Management's Contribution to Structure

Research by Bass 1990 found that 45% to 65% of success or failure was a result of leadership decisions. It is leadership that affords the opportunity to develop the systematic changes that make their way throughout the structure of the organization. They set the systems, structure, and expectations for followers. Managers and supervisors are an extension of that leadership position and are subject to many of the very same constraints. Setting the right expectations is important for the organization and its economic development.

Middle managers are the bridge between executive managers and employees. They are those who interpret information, remove obstacles, motivate employees, make decisions about individual rewards, and clarify paths to goals (Kanter & Stein, 1979). Middle managers are more connected to employees on a personal level and can help them understand the nature of their work environment. Poor management can lead directly to poor employee performance.

In day-to-day operations, employees do not often see their executives. They may attend a meeting or read the newsletter, but they are not personally connected to executives on a human-to-human level in the same way as they are with their managers and supervisors. This proximity and constant interaction encourages relationships which are mutually influencing. Employees take cues from their immediate supervisors and the supervisors take cues from their employees. Eventually they come to a settled agreement about expectations and this becomes the path of operational least resistance. It is an informal process of negotiating between company needs and employee needs.

Since individual managers have their own particular styles, it is important to have diversity on your management team. Not all personalities and styles will appeal to people in the same way. Each individual employee will have their own personal preferences as to whom they connect with the most. If they are in need of direction, they may search out a transactional manager or if they are in need help they can search out the supportive manager. In many cases they may simply talk to the person they connect with or who is most convenient. Each management style has their own particular benefits to the overall functioning of the company.

It is also important to view the organization as a complete functioning entity with specific functional units. It is the multiple approaches used in fulfilling different functions within the organization that helps to create stronger companies. Having a variety of these approaches can raise the overall perception of employees who may view the management team as a connected unit versus individuals with positions maintaining their own unique attributes.

Understanding Subordinate Outcome Needs

Each employee has goals they wish to achieve. These are the reasons they accepted an employment offer. Understanding how these goals fit within the strategic goals of the organization can encourage higher levels of motivation. Employees that find value in company goals through the fulfillment of their personal goals will be consistent in their efforts.

Ultimately, subordinate characteristics determine how a leader's behavior is interpreted within the given work context (Northhouse, 2007). Those with external locus of respond better to directive leadership, while those with internal locus of control respond better to participative management. Knowing which environment you are working and the characteristics of the employees can make a large difference in the success of the leadership style.

For example, an employee with an internal locus of control believes that they are the master of their own fate. They believe that they are in control of their environment and responsible for it. A participative style will encourage them to make a positive influence through their decision-making abilities. Those with an external locus of control feel the world controls their behavior. Such followers need someone to tell them what and when to do it.

Taking a directive management style with professionals with a high internal locus of control is likely to be thwarted and interpreted as unnecessary *chest pounding*. The style of leadership is interpreted as unnecessarily intrusive, discounting of their capabilities, and even insulting to their integrity. An employee with an external locus of control will wait for direction and therefore using a directive approach will provide them with greater understandings of expectations. Expecting externally focused employees to participate their knowledge will take considerable time and effort to re-socialize their behavior.

Subordinate characteristics include the need for autonomy, need for achievement, locus of control, and perceived ability. These function as potential paths for achieving their own positions. For example, employees that have autonomy and an internal locus of control feel they can complete tasks in ways which are most beneficial to them using the skills they have learned best. Each of these perceptual characteristics rests within the individual themselves.

Leaders should understand the nature and characteristics of their employees and develop their structure in ways that encourage maximum performance. Where external locus of control abound, additional role, task and job clarification is needed. Where internal locus of control exists additional job awareness and goal expectations should be defined but the individual methods employees to achieve those goals may be open to foster higher levels of innovation.

Knowing when and where to use directive or participative styles can help in creating additional influence within organizations. It also provides an opportunity in defining how jobs should be structured and the personal latitude employees should have in completing their job functions. Swinging the pendulum too far to the left or right of the employee characteristics will result in lower performance results.

Interrelated Path-Goal Factors

The success of any particular path relies on leadership characteristics, the strength of the strategic plan, market factors, environmental factors and employee characteristics. They can be viewed as follows:

Leadership Characteristics: The personal characteristics of the leader as well as his leadership team. It the ability of these leaders to connect with people, foster trust, articulate vision, and encourage higher levels of performance.

Market Factors: The economic and market factors that influence the success of any strategy in achieving its goals. The strategy should be based on market realities and the needs of customers.

Environmental Factors: Cultural, sociological, team formation, structural, etc… factors that will determine the success of a strategy in its integration within the organization. The environment must be conducive and accepting of the strategy.

Employee Characteristics: The personal abilities of the employees that include emotional, intellect, locus of control, skills, adaptability, maturity, etc… Employees must have the personal capacity to achieve the goals and follow the outline of the strategy.

Once leaders understand these factors they can move to develop appropriate strategies to overcome market difficulties. It is not enough to create a successful strategy without determining how it will work within the different arenas. The leader should understand how he and his team will communicate such strategy, how the market will receive such enhancements, how it is aligned with the structural and cultural aspects of the organization, and whether or not employees currently have the right skills to fulfill the strategy.

Putting together these concepts into a comprehensive strategy takes a considerable amount of experience in organizational processes and human behavior. Each concept should be analyzed to ensure that the strategy is sound and has a higher chance of success. Behavior should match the needs of obtaining support for the proposed strategy in a way that ties people's success to the success of the program.

Within the path-goal theory there are some leadership behaviors that universally help improve employee performance regardless of the style. By creating the right conditions for employees there is a strong likelihood that performance will be improved through clarification. Avoiding confusing messages and contextual influences it is often better to be up-front and concise about what behaviors lead to rewards. According to House, there are a number of leadership behaviors that can make employee needs and preferences contingent on proper performance (1996). These include: clarifying methods of carrying out tasks, clarifying standards, clarifying expectations, and use of rewards.

Employees are often frustrated by the inability to understand the behaviors that lead to success. They talk to each other, socialized in the lunchrooms, and try to make meaning out of their superior's conversations. This role ambiguity can be a strain on goal attainment and create inefficiencies in group behavior. Each person is left to their own devices when trying to create solutions to fulfilling their needs and developing more efficient behavior. Transparency can help them reduce their environmental search efforts and limit poor choices when leadership information is correct and truthful.

A progressive manager can outline his goal and put within place the proper structure to reduce this goal ambiguity the less stress employees are likely to feel and the more efficient the group's activities. Ambiguity is a detracting factor that impacts both males and females equally (DeCaro, 2005). Each gender uses similar cognitive processes when trying to define which actions lead to reward attainment. The more rewards and goals are connected and explained the faster appropriate connections can be made. The leadership strategic functions should provide both the path and the goal in a way that employees can understand and make a connection to their lives and workplace activities.

House and Mitchell (1974) state that leadership strategic functions include the following:

1. Understanding subordinate outcome needs

2. Using incentives to motivate goal attainment

3. Encouraging followers to step forward

4. Clarifying expectations

5. Reduce barriers to connect performance and satisfaction

History of Path-Goal Theory

Prior to the theory much of the research was focused understanding the nature of leadership and follower behavior. The behavior of leaders was believed to influence the overall satisfaction and performance of employees. The results of various studies indicated mixed findings for the connection between leadership and follower behavior.

Evans work in 1970 shed further light on the concept of instrumentalities and expectancies. Accordingly, his research indicated that leader's behavior influenced employee perceptions of proper paths and goals within one organization but not the next. He believed this was related to the organizational context and its influence on these connections.

Research can be traced to the path-goal hypothesis advanced by Georgopoulos, et. al. (1957) and as well as the works of other expectancy-theory researchers. The tenets of this model are that the chance of a certain behavioral response will increase, depending on the expectancies of the outcomes and the personal satisfaction, or valences, which are derived from the outcome.

Victor Vroom discussed this concept in significant detail using his concepts of motivation. He describes motivational performance as a combination of expectancy, instrumentality and valence (Vroom, 1964). Expectancy is the belief that one's performance will lead to a specific outcome, instrumentality is the belief that a person meeting the expectation will earn the reward, and valence is the belief that the rewards are meaningful.

The concept is often written as **Motivational Force (MF) = Expectancy x Instrumentality x Valence.**

Individuals have a choice in taking certain paths to fulfill their goals. This depends in part on what they expect to find, the type of reward the system offers, and whether or not the rewards have significant meaning to the employee. If the three components are in match it should be expected to influence the motivational level of the employee.

Motivation should be matched with appropriate structural paths in order to develop higher levels of performance. When motivation is present but the rewards and paths are absent then there isn't likely to be much behavioral effort. Leadership is about encouraging higher levels of performance through communication, structural adjustments, and the development of clear connections between performance and reward.

Conclusion

Successful strategies take into account the subtle nature of the workplace and develop structures that will encourage higher levels of performance. This performance can only result from employees making appropriate meaning from their environment which leads to the taking of a path of performance that results in reward. That meaning is based within the structure of the organization, the encouragement of their managers, the type of rewards offered, and a level of trust that such rewards will be forthcoming. The more direct the connection between reward and performance the more likely employees will set upon an appropriate course of action. Such associations help employees create motivation as they assess their environment, their abilities, and meaningfulness of the rewards and the likelihood of its attainment. Transformational leaders set this stage by modeling the appropriate behavior and ensuring their strategy moves beyond formal structure to informal structure that impacts the way in which employee envision their environments and place within that environment.

References

Barling, et. al. (2011). Leadership. In s. Zedeck (ED.), APA handbook of industrial and

organizational psychology. Vol 1: Building and developing the organization (183-240).

Washington, DC: American Psychological Association.

DeCaro, N. (2005). An investigation of the relationship of initiating structure, consideration and

gender perception: An examination of the path-goal theory. Capella University, UMI

Dissertations Publishing. Retrieved June 13th, 2013 from ProQuest.

Eagly, A., Johannesen-Schmidt, M., and van E.M. (2003). Transformational,

transactional, and laissez-faire leadership styles: A meta-analysis comparing women and

men. *Psychological Bulletin, 95*, 569–591.

Evans, M. (1970). The effects of supervisory behavior on the path-goal relationship.

Organizational Behavior and Human Performance **5**: 277–298.

Georgopoulous, et. al. (1957). A path-goal approach to productivity. *Journal of Applied

Psychology, 41*: 345-353.

Hernstein, R. (1970). On the law of effect. *Journal of the Experimental Analysis of Behavior, 13*.

House, R. & Mitchell, R. (1974). Path-goal theory of leadership. *Journal of Contemporary

Business*, 3.

House, R. (1996). Path-goal theory of leadership: lessons, legacy, and a reformulated theory.

Leadership Quarterly, 7 (3).

House, R, J., and Mitchell, T. R. (1974). Path-Goal Theory of Leadership. *Journal of

Contemporary Business*, 3, 81-98.

House, R. (1971) A path goal theory of leader effectiveness. *Administrative science quarterly, 16*

(3).

Kim, K., Dansereau, F., Kim, I. S., & Kim, K. S. (2004). A multi-level theory of leadership: The impact of culture as a moderator. *Journal of Leadership and Organizational Studies, 11*(1), 78-93.

Mawhinney, T. & Ford, J. (1977). The path goal theory of leadership effectiveness: an operant interpretation. *Academy of Management Review, 2* (3).

Millenson, I. (1967) *Principles of Behavior Analysis.* New York: Macmillan.

Vandergrift, R. & Matusitz, J. (2011). Path-goal theory: a successful Columbia Records story. *Journal of Human Behavior in the Social Environment, 21* (4).

Northhouse, R. (2007). Leadership (fourth edition). Sage Publications: Thousand Oaks, CA.

Vroom, V. (1964). *Work and Motivation.* New York: Wiley.

The Creation of Leadership

Developing the Leadership Mentality

If your actions inspire others to dream more, learn more,

do more and become more, you are a leader.-John Quincy Adams

The Creation of Leadership

Leadership is an important component that draws people into a shared vision and uses that vision to achieve worthwhile goals. Without shared visions, it is difficult for people to work together and align their actions in ways that build something bigger than themselves. What makes one person a strong leader and one a weak leader is a topic of debate and considers many different factors and viewpoints. It is a question that reaches back in history and has been argued by researchers, lay people, and decision-makers for centuries. Essential leadership is necessary for future growth and collective action.

Serious students of leadership have come to some conclusions that leadership is in part forms of intelligence that includes General Intelligence (IQ), Emotional-Social Intelligence (EQ), and Cognitive Fluidity to help them make proper decisions in tough situations where only ambiguous information is available. Leaders draw road maps where previous road maps may not be found and help others to make those same conclusions. They can bring groups of people to higher levels of achievement through their own understandings and perspectives that encourage togetherness. Thus, leadership is based both in intelligence and social ability.

Leaders cannot work within a vacuum and are socially embedded within organizational and political networks. As they begin to ponder and solve complex problems, others begin to follow their path to achieve their own personal and professional goals. The leader is aware that each person has a certain perspective and level of unfulfilled needs that can be tapped as a resource. By encouraging goal directed behavior through expanded perception of individual need fulfillment within the wider organizational objective fulfillment such leaders are able to raise the synergistic efforts of a group of people to determine a new destiny.

The exceptional nature of such leaders is that as they raise people they also raise social pressure within networks to work toward similar outcomes. It is a slow twist to a productive end. Leadership is a catalyst that connects people to appropriate paths in ways that make sense to the members of a group. When enough people are connected to the path, it is possible to create self-perpetuating growth with its own norms and values that carry the vision into the future outside of the leader's influence. These norms and values maintain the upward trajectory of the group and become embedded into the culture to create new standards. How the social network gets from point A to point B is the strategy and path set by the leader using various traits, skills and environmental cues.

Leaders Think and Act Critically

Critical decision-making is vitally important to accurate assessments and successful strategic implementation. Current leaders have a hard time using their critical thinking skills to solve problems and this trend may continue into the next generation of leaders. This in turn limits their ability to lead others out of difficult situations. Jenkins and Cutchens (2011) have studied the lack of critical thinking in business students and their inability to apply such skills to difficult situations.

An underlying assumption of all leadership is that people use interpersonal skills in the environment to increase self-awareness, understand others, and learn from life's experiences (Burbach, et. al, 2004). Leaders constantly learn about life in order to become more aware of how their behavior influences others and how life's lessons can enhance their decision-making abilities. When their skills consolidate to create higher levels of influential performance they have self-actualized into a leadership persona.

Self-reflection helps to create stronger leadership. Leadership is the ability to reflect on oneself and the events that determine what to believe and which actions to take in certain situations (Ennis, 1993). Without the ability to think about concepts and challenge premises, it is difficult for people to realize new insight and solutions. Leaders require the ability to see beyond surface assumptions and take into consideration human nature if they are to put forward successful strategies that have personal meaning for participants.

Critical thinking affords the opportunity for leaders to use critical reflection, integrate personal experiences, and use learning to engage and understand new ideas that challenge conventional thinking (Reynolds, 1999). It is nearly impossible to break from limited molds unless leaders are willing to challenge and grow the ability of people to achieve new heights. It is a process of helping to think beyond the present.

Such reflection and insight comes with a price. It can often create considerable discomfort and dissonance for both the leader and others (Brookfield, 1994). To think anew means one must give up the old. This requires a level of energy and analysis in order to integrate new concepts within one's life while letting go of those strategies that no longer work. It takes even more courage to project these concepts into the environment in a way that fosters meaningful change.

It is often beneficial to envision critical thinking and leadership from a specific set of awareness criteria. As the leader moves through various experiences, they are better able to envision and incorporate multiple points of view for the greatest impact and effectiveness of action. Actions required to lead critically include:

-Be aware of the context of your situation and evaluate the implications of your decisions.

- Ask questions and listen appropriately.

- Take the time to understand the diversity of others' decisions, values, and opinions.

-Be flexible and open-minded in your decision-making.

- Accept, internalize, and apply constructive criticism.

-Evaluate assumptions before you try to challenge them.

-Understand processes before you try to change them.

-Know the strengths and weaknesses of your followers and direct or empower accordingly.

- Be purposeful and take into account your organization's mission and values when making decisions.

- Engage others where they are, not where you want them to be.

- Encourage critical followership.

- Take informed action.

The study by Jenkins and Cutchens, utilized 80 advanced leadership students to analyze and understand the concept of *leading critically*. It is important to teach students and executives that thinking critically helps one to apply such skills in different situations to enhance leadership. To lead critically requires to both think and act critically. Through the understanding of critical thinking in leadership, higher order leadership skill can be developed.

The study brings to our awareness that effective leadership has at least two parts. One must not only think critically but also act critically to be effective. It is hard enough for people to think for themselves but to then act against the grain of *group think* can be extremely difficult and stressful. Such actions are often thwarted by pressures of social adherence, dissent of opinion, and loss of support. To lead means to chart one's own course and give a path for others to follow.

Leaders Have High Social and General Intelligence

Intelligence and personality are factors in successful leadership development. As organizations become more complex, larger, and multi-national, the leadership team will need to develop and recruit a higher executive skill set. Global leadership requires in part the mastery of cognitive intelligence (IQ), personality, and emotional intelligence (EI). A paper by Colfax, Rivera and Perez (2012), helps explore how emotional intelligence enhances the overall ability of global leaders to influence their organizational environments. Their paper sheds interesting light on the concept that global leaders require certain abilities to be successful in their environment.

Global companies are complex animals that require certain knowledge, skills and abilities (KSA's) to manage well. As these skills grow and develop, other aspects of human development take precedence in order to use these skills and abilities effectively. The emotional-social development of people is a main factor that separates those who will succeed from those who will not succeed in the global management environment.

Emotional intelligence is a concept of how the individual relates to both themselves as well as people within the world. It is the ability to manage the amebic human elements of our social environment. Through understanding oneself, leaders can better understand the needs of others and thereby create more influence within their social networks.

According to Bradberry and Grieves' (2009) survey of 500,000 people, it was discovered that emotional intelligence accounted for 58% of performance and was more predictive than standard intelligence alone. To put the importance of EQ in perspective it was also found that those with high IQ outperformed others 20% of the time while those with high EQ outperform others 70% of the time.

Knowing the importance of EQ in successful global leadership is not the same as knowing how to foster it. Gregersen, Morrison & Black (1999) believes that global leadership is born and not made. In other words, it is enhanced but essential elements must come with the person. Such leaders have certain skills and abilities that when tested within the environment is manifested into greater performance. Through awareness, training and opportunity global leadership skills can come alive and into full bloom.

Colifax, Rivera and Perez contend that limitations on thinking have damaged the field of global leadership in the sense that too much emphasis on the financial bottom line encouraged an over reliance on analytical measures. The complete and well-developed person has emotion and reason to aid them in their cause. In order to manage effectively the multiple personalities, cultures, and systematic management issues in an organization on a global scale requires the use of IQ, personality and EQ. Such leaders can stir the emotions to create systematic developments in the environment in a way that furthers attention and motivation of followers toward key focal points.

Leaders are Adaptive Complex Thinkers

The world is complex and so are the environments that leaders navigate. New environments require leaders to be adaptive and adjust their behaviors to overcome multiple demands. At present, the literature is weak on understanding the theoretical implications of complex leadership styles. The researchers Thatcher, et. al (2013), discuss a model of association between the leader's self-concepts (the mind) and the neuro-scientific basis of this complexity (the brain). They found that complexity of thought, effectiveness, and brain differentiation work together to develop higher leadership behavior.

Because of the increasing ambiguity of world factors, a number of scientists have begun to discuss the adaptive complexity that leaders display in order to make effective decisions (Denison, et. al., 1995). The nature of that complexity of thought is mixed integrally with adaptive decision-making. In this case, adaptation *"refers to the process by which an individual achieves some degree of fit between his or her behaviors and the new work demands created by the novel and often ill-defined problems resulting from changing and uncertain work situations.* (Chan, 2000, pg. 4)"

The ability to think through the varying scenarios and situations to come to proper conclusions is based upon the meta-cognitive deep-seated abilities of the leaders that influence their self-concepts. Over time, these skills create complex mental constructs that are integrated with concepts of self to make it easier for such leaders to make decisions that are more effective and thought out (Lord et al., 2011). It is a process of experiencing that allows deep perception to differentiate key aspects of the environment and then mesh them into a complex and information laden framework. Some may call this the conceptual blend of environmental stimuli.

Adaptive decision-making is a process of self-awareness that allows individuals to see various situations and social influences that weigh on any particular decision (Endsley, 1995). It comes from a development of the concept of *self* that understands the underlining themes of various cultures and how this *self* fits within those cultures. It can traverse the complexities of culture and its various aspects to adjust behavior when the times call for it. It is not a surface skill that's learned by the majority of the population, as it requires an ability to see *self* in time and space and have the following characteristics (Endsley, 1995):

1.) Perceive changes that are occurring in the environment,

2.) Interpret environmental information and integrate it into goals while understanding the implications of those changes on self.

3.) Make predictions of future events and the systems that develop under the new context.

The researcher's model argues that the leader develops a battery of *selves* they can access in any given situation. Those who are not complex will simply not comprehend many aspects of a situation and rely on a single or few concepts of *self* to interpret their environment. A limited self-understanding in various situations means fewer examples to draw on when needed and limited awareness to achieve new heights.

The ability to think complexly with multiple self-constructs is based in the neuro-connections of the brain. Research has indicated that complex concepts do not map themselves to one spot within the brain but to multiple areas (Cacioppo, et. al, 2008). Therefore, those that can draw from multiple areas can think at deeper and richer levels when compared to others. They use multiple areas of the brain to understand the problems they and their organizations are facing.

It is believed that these complex processes of the brain create effective leadership. The prefrontal lobes are responsible for executive control and behavior (Chow & Cummings, 1999). It is in this part of the brain that regulates the internal states as they respond to environmental stimuli. Those that function well processing emotion, stimuli, goal directed behavior, and social awareness are able to succeed in other leadership possibilities. This effectiveness can be displayed under extreme pressure and stress that is often associated with difficult decision making.

As the brain processes information, its complexity will determine what types of memories it can access based upon its neural wiring. These memories and experiences direct behavior. Complex thinkers have complex brains that are able to access multiple parts of their brains, adjust which processes they are using, and find alternative strategies to achieve their objectives. Such brains are seen as the highest form of leadership and human functioning (Smith et al., 1997).

Thatcher, et. al (2013), conducted a study in which 103 military members were used to study the psychological neurological aspects of decision-making. They used an EEG system to determine neural activities within the brain. Participants were given a military scenario in which they would have to create adaptive thinking to make it through appropriately. They found that leaders that are more complex demonstrated greater adaptive thinking, decisiveness, and positive actions as they interacted with task demands in response to increasingly difficult four-part scenarios. The EEG machine showed that such leaders had differentiated activities throughout the brain when solving complex problems and responding to events making them more accurate and effective.

The report furthers the concept that leadership is partly hardwired into the brain and that experience and skill can be used as a method to draw out such leadership. The nature vs. nurture debate becomes more defined as basic neurological process adaptability processes match with experience and skills to create effectiveness in responding to environmental stimuli. The study of the brain and its ability adds to the possibility of selecting those students with the highest possibilities for leadership.

Leaders Maintain Constant Contact with Employees

Research by Dr. Adam Grant highlights how transformational leadership can transcend people's self-interest to fulfill a common purpose. The leader is seen as the enhancer of employee abilities to create stronger performance around a worthwhile vision. His work focuses on understanding how transformational leaders interact with followers to enhance performance and how pro-social perceptions of employees mediate this performance.

The fundamental responsibility of leadership is to motivate their followers to achieve new heights (Vroom & Jago, 2007). Without motivation, there cannot be meaningful and purposeful action. The transformational leader can foster inspiration to rally motivational effort around a vision. Effectiveness comes through the ability to motivate employees to contribute to the process of change. It is a method of tying employees to goals that have impact on their lives and the overall functioning of the organization.

Transformational leaders have behavioral characteristics that encourage success. They can articulate a vision, emphasize collective identities, express confidence and optimism, rely on core values, and push for ideals (House, 1977). Such leaders understand that people must see the future, should work together to achieve that future, can get through the chaos of change, and focus on their essential value systems while trying to navigate the environment. It is a process of adjusting behaviors and then the environment components for a more productive end.

Influence requires the ability to change reality. Creating structural changes in worker's jobs influences their performance (Piccolo, et. al, 2010). When employees can make connections between their goals, paths to performance, desirable rewards, and the vision they can put their behavior within appropriate context. Such behavior and performance creates a higher level of awareness and socializes group behavior which manifests itself in new reinforced group expectations.

Transformational leadership takes on different dimensions to influence the environment. It includes inspirational, idealized influence, intellectual stimulation and individual consideration (Bass, 1985). Such leaders should learn to inspire, influence their environments, create intellectual interest and provide consideration to the needs of their members. Such behaviors help in maintaining progress and development of a network of followers.

When followers are inspired to act toward some goal they can do this through a belief in the ideal. Intellectual stimulation encourages followers to think about such issues, and individual consideration encourages a feeling of individual importance and responsibility within the process. It is a program of social maintenance that helps bring the collective to higher levels of mutual achievement.

Dr. Adam Grant found that transformational leadership contact with followers improved performance and perceptions of pro-social behavior mediated this relationship. It furthers the argument that there is a relationship between leadership, job design and meaning making of employees. Leaders influence the perceptional boundaries between beneficiaries and individual worker actions. Stronger communication skills, leadership skills, and relations between task and performance with end user (i.e. customer) needs influence the perceived success of that leader. The vision is a way for people to see and contextualize their individual parts into and responsibilities.

Allow others to "Think for Themselves"

Most people who have been in the professional fields for some time have come across a situation where a single person uses power and authority with a dominating communication style to push their will on a corporate board, team, or within the workplace. Research by Tost, et. al (2013) discusses some of the pitfalls of doing so and the eventual decline of team performance. As performance declines so does the ability of organizations to generate income through collaborative effort and idea generation.

Politicized workplaces are stressful and are generally unproductive. According to Eisenhardt and Bourgeois (1988), when there is power inequality within the workplace political conflict rises and team performance declines. Teams should be well balanced to ensure that there is equity of power and the ability to discuss concepts openly for better idea generation.

Power should be used to help push good ideas through to create greater productivity. However, when power is used to diminish the brainstorming process the best ideas stay muted in the background. There is a natural propensity for people to defer all major decisions to those that have the formal power. Those that have the formal power do not always know the right answers or have failed to grasp alternative positions. Power, Leadership and Formal Authority can be summed up as follows:

Power: The ability of a person to control outcomes, how people perceive expenses, or push people in certain behaviors (Keltner, et. al, 2003).

Leadership: The ability to influence others to work toward group objectives and goals (Bass, 2008).

Formal Authority: Holding a position that that allows for a specific role within social hierarchy (Peabody, 1962).

Power, leadership, and formal authority maintain the ability to influence the outcomes of the group's decisions. There are times when this can be beneficial once a final decision has been made and concise action is needed. However, preempting or cutting short the decision process may end up costing the organization later in terms of strategic outcome as well as future willingness of employees to express themselves fully.

Open communication within teams is essential in determining of the team's performance (Dionne et. al, 2004). Common knowledge would indicate that the more freethinking employees are the more likely better decisions are made. Strategic decision making requires the ability to perceive and understand the various outcomes. As thoughts build on each other open communication affords a better brain storming session by sharing knowledge.

The authors conclude that the formalization of power into the hand of an individual limits the overall team performance. The leader's subjective perspectives of power lead them to seek additional power derailing the performance process. The more power a leader feels the more their behavior changes and the more people defer to their power. Followers must willingly give up the power for the leader to gain additional influence.

The research is important for avoiding the concepts of "group think" which limits a team's performance. As leaders become more engrained in the perception of their power the more their behavior prompts team members to give up their authority. The end result of such power deference is poor decisions, poor consequences, and potentially disastrous results. Even though it is possible for a single person to break the cycle by asking the right questions the social structure may try and force adherence leading to a lack of empowerment and performance for the whole group.

Emotionally and Socially Intelligent

Researchers have explored different genres of leadership success for considerable time. They have come to some interesting conclusions of what makes one leader more successful over another. Intelligence, cognitive flexibility, and skill have provided only partial explanations. Research by Singh (2013) further lends credibility that leaders with high emotional and social intelligence are capable of influencing organizations to achieve objectives at new levels.

Leadership can be seen as a social skill which encourages strong followership. It is associated with emotional intelligence factors such as attitude, confidence, respect, and trustworthiness (Fehd, 2001). Through positive actions, leaders foster the success of others and encourage beneficial human-to-human relationships. They have the ability to disarm negativity and work toward stronger goal achievement.

Leaders work around a shared vision. It is the selling of this vision that truly helps people to adjust their behaviors toward a specific end. It is often necessary for leaders to engage in collegiality to create collaboration that allows for enough subordinate power to become part of the vision realization process (Singh, 2008). As employees begin to understand the vision and create synergy toward its achievement, releasing additional power can act as both a reward and an efficiency generator.

Leadership is about influencing others. There are many options of power usage but those that can influence others create self-perpetuating growth. Leadership involves the influencing of others to act toward the attainment of a goal through the use of social relations versus simple structural constraints (Hellriegel, et. al., 2006). In such situations, administrative activities should enhance social leadership but not be the foundation of such leadership. When administrative leadership is restrictive and limiting, it runs the risk of discontentment and breakdown.

Superior performance is often seen in the realm of skills but this does not explain in meaningful depth previous success stories. According to Singh & Manser (2008), around two-thirds of competencies linked to superior performance are emotional and social qualities that exist in the realm of self-confidence, persistence, empathy, flexibility, and the ability to work with others. Therefore, leaders can perform when they are cable of understanding and working with the various human elements by relying on their high emotional intelligence.

This leaves some wondering what emotional intelligence is. According to Caruso (1999), emotional intelligence can be clarified as, "…*the ability to use emotions to help you solve problems and live a more effective life. Emotional intelligence without intelligence, or intelligence without emotional intelligence, is only part of a solution. The complete solution is the head working with the heart"* (p. 26). Thinking and emotion work together to create the highest levels of leadership performance and environmental navigation.

EI and social intelligence go together and can be considered a single construct of emotional and social intelligence and come together in the following abilities (Orme & Bar-on (2002):

1.) Understand and express emotions appropriately.

2.) Understand the feelings of others and establish interpersonal relationships.

3.) Cope with new situations and solve problems on a personal and interpersonal nature.

4.) Be optimistic, positive, and self-motivated toward goals.

To test this social leadership concept Singh (2013) used a sample of 474 participants from 200 organizations. The survey included 55 questions that ranked the strength of observable EI characteristics. They found that the following concepts had the highest rankings of leadership:

Communication

Relationships

Trust

Leadership

Empathy

Conflict Management

Professor Singh argues that to move the bottom line of employees from dependency to independence require the ability to bring them into a shared vision of reality. Administrative structures are designed for management/control purposes but interpersonal leadership is designed to bring people willingly into productive actions. The ability to communication, create trust, foster relationships, provide a level of empathy, and manage conflicts as they rise is important for encouraging people to see a more productive perspective. When the emotionally and socially intelligent leader builds relationships around a vision employee satisfaction level rises.

Previous research has indicated the employee satisfaction is the drawing in of employees to fulfill grander purposes for the organization. It is a process of being part of something greater than oneself in an attempt to participate in the bounded rationality of organizational objectives. When employees are drawn as individuals into the success of an organization and can contribute in their own unique ways they can raise their performance and skill levels in a way that can be hedged by leaders to enhance the firm. The positive of leadership is like the catalyzing agent that bridges the gap between the administrative factors and the economic-social needs of the employees.

Fielder's Leadership Model

Leadership is often situational in its effectiveness and outcomes. When a leader's traits match the requirements of a situation a positive result can occur. Fielder's Model of Leadership helps put within proper context how leadership traits mix with a motivational type to determine the effectiveness of a leader within a particular contextual situation. Crises situations call for one approach while periods of rest require another to develop maximum optimal behavior.

Fielder's model of leadership is one the oldest leadership models available. The performance of a leader depends on two interrelated factors: 1) the degree to which the situation gives the leader control and influence-that is, the likelihood that the leader can successfully accomplish the job; and 2) the leader's basic motivation-that is, whether self-esteem depends primarily on accomplishing the task or on having close supportive relationships with others (Axtell, 1991).

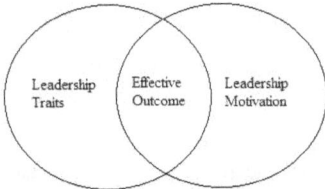

Fielder's Model of Leadership

Fielder believed that individuals have a single leadership style that maintains consistently throughout their lives. This includes either relationship orientation or task orientation. Each style influences how leaders act and solve problems that make them successful. The style does not necessarily take into account those people who can be either task or relationship orientated depending on the situation and their level of skill mastery.

Crisis Leaders

Under high stress situations, some leaders focus on relationships which can cause improper decisions based upon a misalignment of the leadership style to the pace of the crisis (Fiedler and Garcia, 1987). Relationship developing is a slow process while action during a crisis is needed immediately. During a crisis situation the focus on tasks is more effective than a relationship approach. Overcoming a crisis requires quickly executed tasks that accomplish specific goals to overcome the problem. Relationships and the social subtleties that make up those relationships temporarily go on the *back-burner* until the crisis is over.

Peace Time Leaders

In low stress situations, the relationship orientated approach is more important in accomplishing organizational objectives. It is relationships that create social cohesion and togetherness in managing an organization. According to Gannon (1982), relationship leaders are effective when 1.) Leader-member relationships are strong, 2.) the task is unstructured, and 3.) when positional power is weak. Such leadership flourishes in highly intellectual organizations where freedom of thought is needed to be productive.

As task oriented focus or people oriented focus are considered relatively stable traits that exist over a person's lifetime, it is necessary to choose the right style of leader to handle difficult situations. *"In Fiedler's model, leadership effectiveness is the result of interaction between the style of the leader and the characteristics of the environment in which the leader works."* (Gray & Starke, 1988). In other words, the situation and the leadership traits must match for optimal performance. When the environment requires one style of leadership over another it would not be wise to use an inflexible leadership style that relies too heavily on one method.

It is important to remember that effective leadership is not gender specific. Research has lent credibility to the concept that the Contingency Model of leadership applies to both males and females equally (Rice, Bender, & Vitters, 1982). The right leader for a situation is more closely akin to the personality style of that leader versus any physical characteristics. As a culture we may associated certain characteristics with gender but these are social constructions.

In today's world, the concept of leadership has expanded to include new forms, models and people. Fielder's Contingency Model still stands as one of the central lenses to understanding and predicting the effectiveness of future leadership styles in both the workplace and crisis situations. It is through understanding these models and traits that organizational decision makers can develop and place appropriate leaders to handle specific difficult situations. Organizations should seek the right leader for the situation at hand.

Displaying Traits and Behaviors

Making sense out of leadership literature can be difficult. Sometimes using a meta-analysis of other people's research can help in creating stronger understanding. Derue, et. al. (2011) reviews the need to integrate leadership into a more cohesive framework by testing four concepts of leader effectiveness, group performance, follower job satisfaction and satisfaction of leadership. Understanding how traits and behaviors match to create effectiveness is important for determining the overall abilities of the leader to meet goals.

Leadership effectiveness is predicted from the demographics, personality traits, skills and abilities of the leader (Eagly, et. al., 1995). The combination of these factors meshed together into leadership behavior may be most successful. Therefore, successful leadership relies on both behavior and traits to be effective.

Leadership behavior creates overall effectiveness (Judge & Piccolo, 2004). Behavior is most often goal-oriented in the sense that it focused on specific outcomes that seek manifest a vision the leader has. Without action there cannot be change within the environment or movement toward higher forms of performance.

Leadership can be categorized into traits or behaviors (Bass & Bass, 2008; Derue, et. al., 2011)

Traits: demographics, task competence, and interpersonal attributes.

Behaviors: task processes, relational dynamics or change.

Traits are inherent within the individual and can be enhanced or learned over time. Behaviors are the outward actions that focus on the completion of goal seeking behavior. These are the tasks one completes on a daily basis, the activities of other they engage with or the behavioral activity focused on change. When the traits are matched with certain behaviors they create effective leadership.

The researchers Derue, et. al. (2011) reviewed 13 meta-analysis and 46 primary studies to find patterns toward model integration. It was their way of systematically analyzing previous research to determine how effective leadership developed. Leadership traits like conscientiousness appeared to have the highest predictive value for effectiveness. When leadership traits were matched with task competence effectiveness appeared to be higher. Interpersonal attributes were associated with relationship-oriented behavior that increased employee satisfaction. Where task competence and interpersonal attributes matched, there was a higher degree of change oriented action. As expected the "do nothing" or passive leaders were least effective in their styles.

The findings further our understanding that leadership traits pair with behaviors to create effectiveness. Leaders are likely to rely on both innate and learned traits to direct their goal seeking behavior. It is this goal directed behavior that creates task completion that results in effectiveness. It is a life-long process of development where traits and successful behaviors match to make the dynamic combo many leaders seek. How that is manifested in terms of being people or task oriented will determine the type of leadership style used. Despite these preferences leaders still have the ability to use both as the situation demands to be more effective.

Leaders are Learners

Learning organizations are likely to be more successful in developing new products and strategies to compete on the open market. Research by Michie & Zumitzavan (2012), furthers the argument that those organizations that foster learning and are managed by learning leaders are more successful than those who are reactive and focused on pathological styles. Learning leadership is progressive, open-minded, humanistic, and goal orientated approach that results in higher firm development and profits.

Leadership and learning are two components that come together to foster development. The way in which leaders learn has an impact on how they act as administrators. Those that engaged in all four learning styles action, thinking, feeling and assessing others are more capability of using multiple leadership styles such as challenging, inspiring, enabling, modeling, and encouraging (Brown and Posner, 2001).

Learning is one way in which organizations can continually renew themselves versus accepting the fate of a rigid decline. According to Johnson and Scholes, (2002), organizations that are willing to continue learning throughout their lifecycles become more sustainable in the sense that they can adjust to new market trends, structures, and realities. If such organizations are not willing to learn and change they will be eventually crushed under new market realities by more competitive and nimble organizations.

Publically available leaders have the influence to prime the behavior of their followers. When leaders have a healthy respect for learning they can influence the expectations and behaviors of managers who further impact the social structure of employees. Creating a culture that respects and fosters learning, helps in enhancing employees' abilities and the ability of the organization to adapt to market changes.

The researchers Michie & Zumitzavan (2012), attempted to see how the attributes of managers impacted the learning and leading styles that influence organizational success. Twenty North Taiwanese firms were selected for the overall interviews and questionnaires. They found that there was no relationship between learning styles and the demographics of the organization or location. In other words, learning leadership is not tied to organizational demographics. The impact of organizational learning styles was influenced by the leadership styles within the organization.

Effective Organizations: Managers within effective organizations believe that technology and cost reduction were two important factors. However, they agreed that by developing employees skills their organizations performance could be enhanced. Thus, they sent people to seminars, workshops, training, educational outlets, etc... to improve their skills. They welcomed open opinions, managed workplace problems progressively, delegated for employee enhancement, and continued to forecast the needs of their organizations into the future.

Less Effective Organizations: Less effective organizations are marked by their short-sighted thinking that focused on day-to-day issues. They were less able to forecast the future of the organization or able to solidify the goals of the organization. They rarely sent people for enhancement training or education and did not do well in managing employee problems. Furthermore, they were not willing to delegate authority and did not encourage employee opinions.

The research results indicate that short-sighted behaviors, where individuals are not learning stronger actions, are more prone to poor performance. With such results it is important to understand how training and development has an enhanced place in the most successful organizations. Such training doesn't need to be formal but does need to encourage constant learning and development to be effective. The learning style of the leaders and their level of expectation setting appear to foster organizational learning.

Participative or Directive Styles

A study of 445 lecturers and 138 principles sought to determine the satisfaction level of college staff with leadership use of directive or supportive management styles. Research by Awan, et. al. (2011) helps define how college management perception is influenced by employee's locus of control. Even though the results support the general theory's premises it does indicate that extremes of participative or directive leadership behavior can have a negative impact on the functioning of the organization.

Locus of control relates to the belief that either the person or the environment is responsible for personal influence. A person who has an internal locus of control believes that they have influence over the environment while a person with an external locus of control believes that the environment has control over them. This interpretation of the self within the environment impacts behavioral choices one makes and their motivation level.

The research question is, "*What is the relationship between locus of control and subordinates' outcomes, who work under directive and participative leaders, holding constant the effect of principals' role ambiguity and stress?*" In other words, how does internal and external locus of control influence subordinate performance under directive or participative leaders.

The study focused on college professors, assistant professors, associate professors, and lecturers in Pakistan. Leadership behavior and subordinate characteristics were assessed through questionnaires. Three aspects of directive leadership and participative leadership were used during the assessment ranging from low to high.

The study found that directive leadership was associated with leader acceptance by those with an external locus of control and less accepted by people with internal locus of control. Likewise, the study found that a moderate participative leadership had a positive impact on job expectancies of those with an internal locus of control. When leadership was highly supportive it negatively impacted the satisfaction of employees that maintained an external locus of control.

The results generally support path-goal theory in colleges. However, the extremes of leadership appear to be an issue here. Too much of a good thing appears to create lower satisfaction among employees. Too high directive and too high participative leadership styles appear to negatively impact their environments. The key may be to balance these extremes based upon the pendulum of locus of control found among employees within the organization. Some employees may need to be told what to do while others drawn into the management decisions.

Supporting Themselves with Different Types of Power

Leadership and power work together to influence organizational activities. According to Goncalves (2013), future leaders will need to understand how to define their leadership style, use that leadership style in alignment with existing organizational contexts be able to tell stories that create a vision, and tap into their imaginations to find solutions. This leadership is defined by the necessity of developing a stronger management platform for a more complex world.

The use of power can be legitimate or illegitimate. In general, legitimate power supports a governing system in the betterment of a wider group of people. Illegitimate power focuses more on self-serving ends outside of a proper governing system. Generally these are established through culture and governing laws. In the case of the workplace such power should be used to influence people to fulfill organizational objectives in ways that are fair and appropriate. When such power is overly coercive it can detract from the organizational mission and from the governing system itself.

There are seven forms of power that are used to create influence:

Legitimate Power: The power of a formal position.

Expert Power: Knowledge based power.

Coercive Power: The power of fear.

Reward Power: The ability to give or take away awards.

Referent Power: The power of knowing and referring to powerful people.

Information Power: It is the power that comes from the use of information.

Each of these power sources has the ability to influence some situations but can lack effectiveness in other situations. For example, reward power can encourage higher levels of performance but coercive power might be more effective in chaotic situations. Referent power may get you a job but expert power is more effective in performance. When and where to use each of these powers, is dependent on the situation and context of the environment.

Understanding the different types of power used within organization and the preferred power of the leader helps to understand better methods of not only gaining power within organizations but also how to manage the organization itself. Relying too heavily on one type can limit the ability of the organization to create different types of pressures and rewards to ensure the highest amount of performance. Power is not necessarily a bad or good thing but is a natural part of living in a social world. Some are more egalitarian than others but ultimately each can be used appropriately to maintain forward momentum.

Conclusion

Leadership is seen as existing in three different spheres that interrelate to each other. The three constructs are traits, behaviors, and environments. Some leaders who have the right traits will need the influence of an education to display those behaviors most advantageous for goal attainment. Other leaders have the right traits but neither their environment nor learned behavior will allow them to become leaders. Sometimes leaders may have both the traits and behavior but the environment is not conducive to their particular style. Only when the three factors are in alignment is it possible to see high levels of leadership.

Traits: Traits are those factors inherent within the person's biological nature and personality. Leaders have traits that help them to be critical thinkers, open minded, inquisitive, adaptive, socially aware, intelligent, emotionally developed, and able to communicate. The fundamental seeds of development must already be present.

Behaviors: Behaviors are actions based on internal and external stimuli. Leaders engage in behaviors that draw employees into a vision, goal directed, productive, inclusive, participative or directive, positive, consistent, and vision formulating. Using existing traits and enhancing their behavioral effectiveness over a lifetime can encourage higher levels of leadership.

Environment: Behaviors live within the right circumstances and conditions that make their traits and behaviors effective. Leaders exist in an environment that is receptive to their traits and behaviors. Crises need different leadership styles than during peacetime. Effective leadership styles are often based on the situation, power structures of society, and cultural value systems of society.

Traits, behaviors and the environment work together to forge a universal value system that applies to humans beyond their cultural backgrounds. According to Peterson & Seligman, (2004) an analysis of cultures, religion, moral philosophers and others have revealed some universal values leaders should have:

Wisdom: The cognitive ability to be creative, love of learning, judgment, curiosity, and perspective.

Courage: Emotional strengths to accomplish goals in the face of resistance that include bravery, perseverance, honesty and zest.

Humanity: The interpersonal skills that include love, kindness and social intelligence.

Justice: Community approaches that strengthen society through teamwork, fairness, and leadership.

Temperance: The skills to avoid excess, forgiveness, humility, prudence, self-regulation.

Transcendence: The strengths that connect to a larger universe that includes appreciation of beauty and excellence, gratitude, hope, humor, spirituality.

Leadership is complex and requires a lifetime to master due to the multitude of blended factors. Many of the skills leaders learn start out in childhood and begin to manifest themselves later in life when significant experience is gained. Some are naturally more prone to be leaders than others and this is not dependent on socio-economic status. A receptive environment within organizations can help develop those leadership styles that are sure to be needed in the future as organizations compete in highly dynamic environments. Enhancing personal strengths throughout one's career can foster those aspects of leadership that are likely to work for the individual. Once mastered, these skills must meet a receptive environment creating the ultimate leadership gamble. At one time in place where a style works well does not mean that it will work well in all other areas.

References

Axtell, R. (1991). *Gestures: the do's and taboos of body language around the world*. NY: John Wiley & Sons.

Avolio, J., Walumbwa, F. & Weber, T. (2009). Leadership: Current theories, research, and future directions. *Annual Review of Psychology, 60*, 421 – 449.

Awan, et. al, (2011). Locus of control as moderator of relationship between leadership behaviors of principles and their faculty outcomes: a path-goal approach. *International Journal of Social Sciences & Education, 1* (4).

Barbuto, J. (2005). Motivation and transactional, charismatic, and trans-formational leadership: A test of antecedents. *Journal of Leadership and Organizational Studies, 11*.

Bartlett, C. & Ghoshal, S. (1992). What is a global manager? *Harvard Business Review* (September-October), 124 – 132.

Bass ,B & Bass, R. (2008). *TheBass handbook of leadership: Theory, research, and managerial applications*. New York, NJ: Free Press.

Bass, B. (1985) *Leadership and performance beyond expectations.* New York: Free Press.

Bradberry, T. & J. Greaves (2009).*Emotional intelligence 2.0.* California: Talent Smart

Brookfield, S. D. (1994). *Understanding and facilitating adult learning: A comprehensive analysis of principles and effective practices*. San Francisco: Jossey-Bass and England: Open University Press.

Brown, M. and Posner, Z., (2001). Exploring the relationship between learning and leadership. *Leadership and organizational development journal, 22* (5–6), 274–280.

Burbach, M. E., Matkin, G. S., & Fritz, S. M. (2004). Teaching critical thinking in an introductory

    leadership course utilizing active learning strategies: A confirmatory study. *College Student*

    Journal, 38(3), 482-493.

Cacioppo, J. et. al. (2008). Neuroimaging as a new tool in the toolbox of psychological science. *Current*

    Directions in Psychological Science, 17, 62–67.

Caruso, D. & Salovey, P. (2003). *The emotionally intelligent manager.* San Fransisco: Jossey-Bass.

Caruso, D., Mayer, J., & Salovey, P. (2002). Emotional intelligence and emotional leadership. In R. E.

    Riggio, S. E. Murphy, & F. J. Pirozzolo (Eds.), *Multiple intelligences and leadership* (pp. 55 –

    74). Mahwah, NJ: Lawrence Erlbaum.

Chan, D. (2000). Understanding adaptation to changes in the work environment: Integrating individual

    difference and learning perspectives. *Research in Personnel and Human Resources*

    Management, 18, 1–42.

Chow, T., & Cummings, J. L. (1999). *Frontal-subcortical circuits.* In B. L. Miller & J. L. Cummings

    (Eds.), The human frontal lobes: Functions and disorders (pp. 3–26). New York, NY: Guilford

    Press.

Colfax, R., Rivera, J. & Perez, K. (2010). Applying Emotional Intelligence (EQ-I) in the workplace:

    vital to global business success. *Journal of International Business Research, 9.*

Denison, D. (1995). Paradox and performance: Toward a theory of behavioral complexity in managerial

    leadership. *Organization Science, 6,*524–540

Derue, D., et. al. (2011). Trait and behavioral theories of leadership: an integration and meta-analytic

    test of their relative validity. *Personnel Psychology, 64* (1).

Dionne, et. al (2004). Transformational leadership and team performance. Journal of Organizational

    Management, 17: 177–194.

Eagly A., et. al. (1995). Gender and the effectiveness of leaders: A meta-analysis. *Psychological Bulletin, 117*, 125–145.

Eisenhardt, K. & Bourgeois, L. (1988). Strategic decision making in high-velocity environments: Toward a midrange theory. Academy of Management Journal, 31: 737–770.

Endsley, M. (1995b). Toward a theory of situation awareness in dynamic systems. *Human Factors, 37*, 32–64.

Ennis, R. H. (1993). Critical thinking assessment. *Theory into Practice, 32*(3), 179-186.

Fehd, L. 2001. *Emotional intelligence: An executive handbook*. Austin: Good Pages.

Fiedler, F. and Garcia, J. (1987) *New Approaches to Leadership, Cognitive Resources and Organizational Performance*, New York: John Wiley and Sons.

Goncalves, M. (2013). Leadership styles: the power to influence others. *Journal of Business & Social Science, 4* (4).

Graen, G.& Uhl-Bien, M. (1995). Relationship-based approach to leadership: Development of leader-member exchange (LMX) theory of leadership over 25 years: Applying a multi-level multi-domain perspec-tive. *Leadership Quarterly, 6.*

Grant, B. (2012). Leading with meaning: beneficiary contact, prosocial impact, and the performance effects of transformational leadership. *Academy of Management Journal, 55* (2).

Gregersen, H., A. Morrison & J. Black (1999, November). What makes Savvy global leaders? *Ivey Business Journal, 64*(2), 44. Retrieved October 9, 2008, from Business Source Complete database.

Filley, A. & House, R. (1969). *Managerial process and organizational behavior*. Glenview Il; Scott Foresman.

Gannon, M. (1982). *Management: An Integrated Framework*. Boston: Little, Brown.

Gray, Jerry L., and Frederick A. Starke. *Organizational Behavior: Concepts and Applications*.

    Columbus, Ohio: Merril.

Hellriegel, D., Jackson, S.E., Slocum, J., Staude, G., Amos, T., Klopper, H.B., Louw, L. & Oosthuizen,

    T. (2006). *Management*. Oxford: Cape Town.

House, R. J. 1977. A 1976 theory of charismatic leadership. In J. G. Hunt & L. L. Larsen, (Eds.),

    Leadership: The cutting edge: 189–207. Carbondale: Southern Illinois University Press.

Jenkins, D. & Cutchens, A. (2011). Leading critically: a grounded theory of applied critical thinking in

    leadership studies. *Journal of Leadership Education, 10* (2).

Johnson, G. and Scholes, K.,(2002). *Exploring corporate strategy*. Essex: Pearson Education.

Judge, T. A., & Piccolo, R. F. (2004). Transformational and transactional leadership: A meta-analytic

    test of their relative validity. *Journal of Applied Psychology, 89*, 755 – 768.

Judge T, & Piccolo R.. (2004). Transformational and transactional leadership: A metaanalytic test of

    their relative validity. *Journal of Applied Psychology, 89*, 755–768.

Keltner, et. al. (2003). Power, approach, and inhibition. Psychological Review, 110: 265–284.

Kinicki, A. & Kreitner, R. (2009). *Organizational Behavior: Key concepts, skills & practices* (fourth

    edition). McGraw-Hill Company.

Lord, et. al. (2011). A framework for understanding leadership and individual requisite complexity.

    Organizational Psychology Review, 1,104–127.

Michie, J. & Zumitzavan, F. (2012). The impact of learning and leadership management styles on

    organizational outcomes: a study of Tyre Firms in Thailand. *Asia Pacific Business Review, 18*

    (4).

Orme, G. & Bar-On, R. 2002. The contribution of emotional intelligence to individual and

    organizational effectiveness. *Competency and Emotional Intelligence, 9*, 23-28.

Peabody, R. (1962). Perceptions of organizational authority: A comparative analysis. *Administrative Science Quarterly, 6:* 463–482.

Peterson, C., & Seligman, M. E. P. 2004. The VIA Classification of Character Strengths. Retrieved from http://www.viacharacter.org/www/en-us/viainstitute/classification.aspx

Singh, P. (2013). A collegial approach in understanding leadership as a social skill. *International business & economics research journal, 12* (5).

Piccolo, et.al. (2010). The relationship between ethical leadership and core job characteristics. *Journal of Organizational Behavior,* 31: 259–278.

Rice, R., Bender, L., Vitters, A. (1982). Testing the validity of contingency model for female and male leaders. *Basic & Applied Social Psychology, 3* (4).

Reynolds, M. (1999). Critical reflection and management education: Rehabilitating less hierarchical approaches. *Journal of Management Education, 23*(5), 537-53.

Rockstuhl, et. al. (2011). Beyond General Intelligence (IQ) and Emotional Intelligence (EQ): The Role of Cultural Intelligence (CQ) on Cross-Border Leadership Effectiveness in a GlobalizedWorld. *Journal of Social Issues, 67 (4),*

Singh, P. & Manser, P. (2008). Correlation between the perceived emotionally intelligent interpersonal behaviors of school principals and the job satisfaction of their teachers. *The International Journal of Knowledge, Culture & Change Management, 8*(1), 189-200.

Smith, et. al. (1997). *Building adaptive expertise: Implications for training design strategies.* In M. A. Quinones & A. Ehrenstein (Eds.), Training for a rapidly changing workplace (pp.89–118). Washington, DC: American Psychological Association. doi:10.1037/10260-004

Thatcher, et. al. (2013). The psychological and neurological bases of leader self-complexity and effects on adaptive decision-making. *Journal of Applied Psychology, 98* (3).

Tost, et. al. (2013). When power makes others speechless: the negative impact of leader power on team performance. Academy of Management Journal, 56 (5).

Triandis, H. C. (2006). Cultural intelligence in organizations. *Group and Organization Management, 31*, p. 20 – 26.

Trepanier, et. al (2012). Social and motivational antecedents of perceptions of transformational leadership: a self-determination theory perspective. *Canadian Journal of Behavioral Science, 44* (4).

Vroom, V. H., & Jago, A. G. 2007. The role of the situation in leadership. *American Psychologist,* 62: 17–24.

Leadership Strategy Development

Knowing What to Say, How to Say It, and When to Say It.

All men can see these tactics whereby I conquer,

but what none can see is the strategy out of which victory is evolved.-Sun Tzu

Strategy Development

Strategy is a chosen path to achieve organizational and personal goals. The development of strategy is as much a cognitive process as it is a creation of a plan that navigates organizational difficulties. It uses environmental data to formulate plans that effectively solves problems as well as engages others in that solution generation process. These goal oriented frameworks should be rooted in the culture and values of the company without neglecting outside stakeholders. It is a process of research, thought formulation, and social projection that encourages the highest levels of employee engagement.

Each organizational decision-maker comes with past personal and professional experiences they use to weigh and judge strategic decisions. Their perception and selective attention will impact what they see within the environment and what actions the organization can take. Considering multiple vantage points will help leaders balance out their limited perspective with critical judgment needed for success.

Ultimately, all strategies must fit within the cognitive frameworks and schemata of employees. Failure to take into account their perspectives may limit the success of implementation through employee and stakeholder resistance. A strategy should bind people to the required action and make it meaningful for each participant. Every person within the strategy should feel that they have an important part in the organization's success.

Once strategies are formulated they need to be carefully implemented throughout the organization. Implementation is one of the most complex and confusing aspects of strategy formation. Executives often ignore the multitudes of practical implementation information in the formation process. They set the path but fail to understand the nuances of each step required to walk that path.

It is beneficial to think of strategy as purposeful evolution of an organization. As the organization begins to adjust itself within the environment it will need to ensure that all components are also brought into alignment. This is typically done through finding basic strategic approaches and adjusting the inner workings of the organization to those approaches. Each employee is encouraged to be brought into the fold of development to meet defined goals.

Strategy in Small and Medium Organizations

Strategy formation may be one of the most important aspects of managing a company. Without a proper strategy the ship bounces around the sea in hopes of finding fruitful land. How that strategy is formed is often a difficult question to answer. Research by Pop and Borza, (2013) helps to determine how strategy works within small and medium organizations (SME). This helps further solidify the concept that strategy is based upon the environment and resources available that help make companies more competitive.

In developing strategy it is important for managers to interpret the signals coming from the internal and external environment appropriately. Doing so creates an opportunity to formulate strategies not only for their daily operations but also for long term corporate interests. It is this understanding that will act as a guide to regeneration and renewal that leads to corporate achievement.

Successful strategies are developed, implemented and then re-evaluated. Companies that are static and unable to change are the ones that eventually suffer economic decline. Renewing products, procedures, marketing campaigns, distribution methods, financial resources, and human capital components are just some of the overall process that should be revisited and improved on a continual basis.

To help determine how strategy is evaluated, formulated and implemented at Romanian SMEs the researchers conducted a number of case studies. They utilized five companies and formulated their approaches into concepts such as the definition of strategy, implementation, development, references, evaluation, and information in the strategic process. The study helps highlight the process of strategic development as well as the thought processes that are applied.

Understanding the environment and moving through a systematic evaluation of strengths and weaknesses is beneficial. The process of environmental and competitive understanding is seen as "keeping an eye on the market". The decision makers used exact data to make their strategies but maintained a level of flexibility to mitigate risk. They adjusted their strategy when the market called for it.

When companies are developing the mission the management team's personal values are extremely important in developing appropriate statements and policies. Missions and processes have changed overtime making strategy a fluid endeavor. There wasn't a specific point at which the companies made changes but they did so based upon their understanding of when environment has changed. This process doesn't end throughout the life of the organization.

When change was needed it was typically the manager or the executive that made the decision. They focused on changing processes to adjust the internal workings of the organization to newly adopted strategies. At times these changes created a positive or negative chain reaction throughout the organization. When these changes became dysfunctional they changed the plan again to bring them to a more positive outcome that more closely reflected what is need to be successful in the market.

Since a majority of new companies went bankrupt the managers tried to maintain an entrepreneurial stance and used strategy to ensure they are meeting their longer term objectives. This included trying new products and services to create new opportunities. Yet despite their interest, the new opportunities needed to fit within their strategic needs to be considered relevant.

Each company used their own specific approaches to formulating a strategy. The report doesn't go into these concepts in depth but it is possible to see some trends that include 1.) understanding environmental needs, 2.) understanding internal resources, 3.) developing the strategy, 4.) changing processes to match the strategy, 5.) being open to new opportunities within the strategy and, 6.) changing the strategy when the market changes. As such, strategy is a constant fluid evaluation of one's internal and environmental factors. It is a process of seeing the trends and meeting those trends in ways that maximize financial growth and organizational sustainability.

Corporate Market Strategies

As the market becomes chaotic the ability to change the strategic formation models becomes a necessity to match this need. Strategic behavior is associated with capital resources and the competencies of the corporation. A paper by EL Namiki in the Ivey Business Journal (2013) helps in furthering the Systemic Strategy Analysis Model (SSAM) of strategic thinking which focuses on the flows of thought formation within companies in order to analyze a company's competitive position.

Strategic behavior is seen as a process of developing and enacting choices. Systematic strategic behavior focuses more on the developing and enacting of choices that are in alignment with the structural and environmental constraints of an organization. Strategic business choices, by their nature, are more confined than those enacted by individuals. Proper analysis is needed to define the possibilities and accuracy of strategy.

Where resources and company attributes meet each other there is a potential strategy that can be developed. When the attributes and resources change there would be a shift in the overall strategic trajectory. The path would adjust based upon the most advantageous route to achieving objectives. It is possible to map these concepts and draw out possible strategies. Consider the following four concepts when developing a strategy:

Seeking Concentration: Concentration relates to the overall concept of market saturation. When a small amount of firms dominate an industry, it is said to have high concentration. If a large amount of entrepreneurial or boutique firms exist within an industry, there is a low level of concentration. The success of achieving a level of market presence will depend on the ability to meet the challenges of the environment based upon competing companies.

Seeking Competencies: Competency is a level of strong and competitive performance in a particular domain. It could be anything that furthers a strategy such as distribution, product design, technology, etc. Organizations seeking to enhance a competency either hire the right people or train them with competitive skills. Successful firms like Google have attracted the right talent to further their strategic competencies.

Seeking Focus: At times it is necessary for companies to narrow down their efforts and focus on core offerings in order to enhance those things they excel at and remove activities they cannot.

This may mean selling off brands that do not enhance core competencies or outsourcing internal functions that distract from the core competencies. Improving upon core competencies creates higher levels of competitive advantage.

End Game: When a company has maximized profits and a period of low profits sets into product lines or services they should consider an end game. This end game occurs when competitive offerings decline and there is little hope of recovery or the products have lost their market luster. Generally, this is a result of root misalignment between the offerings and current market needs. A strategy should include when to get out of the market and move onto new products and services.

Strategic Development as a Social and Logical Process

What is rationality strategy? According to a paper by Schaefer, et. al (2013) rationality is an interpersonal communication skill beyond subject knowledge. There is a differentiation between emancipative communication and strategic thinking. The researchers studied the prefrontal and parietal brain regions that are associated with strategic and communicative reasoning according to the theory of communicative action. They found that there are two different processes at place when discussing strategic reasoning and social emotional cognitions. Each has their own neural connections that determine actual strategies and the possible effectiveness of those strategies.

The theory of communicative reasoning by Jurgen Habermas focuses on either success oriented strategic action or social understanding oriented communicative action. Strategic action in this theory is the manipulation of others while communicative reasoning seeks to harmonize actions between the person and their social environment by using language and semantics. They use two different reasoning functions and impact the strategic choices of leaders.

Rationality has both a social and a logical side. Communicative reasoning is collaborative and strategic reasoning is goal oriented. Each is a means to an end but one takes into consideration the moral dilemmas created through decisions while the other seeks gains regardless of the human outcome. The way in which a person approaches the environment determines the type of logic they are using and where it is based within the neural connections of the brain.

The research on social perceiving is important because it can help us determine how leaders make decisions strategically. As one uses pure logic without moral reasoning they activate a different set of brain functions to make those determinations. However, by using moral reasoning and an alternative set of brain functioning they can consider such things as the cost of human life or appropriate impact on individuals. Leaders should earn to use strategy and morality together to maximize their impact.

Moral judgments and the ability to see these moral dilemmas is a precursor to appropriate judgment. Pure strategy without moral judgment is considered anti-social by nature and doesn't take into account the needs of people that the strategy influences. One can think of the psychopath who is strategically accurate in short-term gains but fails to have empathy and consideration over those whom the decisions impacts. Leadership and strategy should not be inhumane, cold, calculating, or abusive to others but should instead seek a collaborative maximum gain.

In their study, Schaefer, et. al (2013) studied the brains of individuals as they judged different real life scenarios from a communicative reasoning or strategic perspective. The far majority of participants were able to judge between the two types of approaches. They found that communicative reasoning activated a network of brain areas including the temporal poles, STS, and precuneus. Strategic reasoning also showed less activation in these areas of the brain when compared to communicative reasoning.

The argument furthers the concept that strategy has both an economic and a social aspect. Pure strategic thinking is about creating gain in the market regardless of its consequences on others while communicative reasoning takes into consideration moral concepts. Well balanced strategy should process from the two strategic methods in order to understand the pure logic of decisions but also the moral consequences of such decisions. As most of our world and environment is made of social interpretations and interaction it is this process of considering the possibilities of cooperation that further logical strategic success.

Thinking Outside the Bounds

Game theory is one way to see how actions with other players can influence the outcome. The theory is a genre of mathematics that attempts to calculate potential outcomes based upon the movement of other players. Since markets have limited sizes and require competition Game Theory is one way to envision the overall to effective strategy and its development.

Reviewing a number of game theory results the authors Crawford, Costa-Gomes, and Iriberri (2013) discuss why people often deviate systematically from equilibrium in game theory. By understanding why some choices appear irrational (level-k) it is possible to better determine under what circumstances such behavior is prevalent.

Strategic thinking is a natural part of everyone's life and people develop strategies to obtain needed resources. In game theory each person seeks to maximize their payoffs based upon predicting the choices of others by assuming the rationality of the other players. This is called bounded rationality as all players work under the same assumptions.

There is also something called level-k responses or L0. It is an assumption that all players beliefs will improve in an attempt to take the dominant stance that eventually leads to equilibrium. A level-k response would indicate that a person is making decisions outside of shared understandings as well as a "rational" choice. This level highlights the person's cognitive model and assumptions of the game may be different than other players.

Because there is a lack of information when a game starts, some players recognize this ambiguity and avoid dominant positions that often fit within the equilibrium model. Each person responds to the game with a personality type that impacts the types of decisions they are willing to make. It is their personal beliefs that help them develop a strategy for dealing with the components of a game and choosing certain patterns.

Equilibrium is seen as rationality with a common belief among players. The more evidence a person obtains from the game the more accurate and rational their decisions. Players often make larger and wilder maneuvers in the beginning of a game and then move to defined choices toward the later part of the game as they begin to understand the rules and strategies of their opponents.

Using a concept called level-k models it is possible to see how certain behaviors move away from equilibrium choices and under what circumstances such behavior can be expected. Many poor decisions may be made from a lack of time, information, or cognitive deficiencies.

Yet it is possible to find that level-k decision making may have some advantages in resolving games and conflict that "rational" choices do not have.

In a level–k decision it is believed that the player is making decisions regardless of the other players within the game. Level-1 players have higher cognitive hierarchies and believe others are playing at level-o. As one moves up the cognitive complexity level of making strategic choices they often erroneously make assumptions that other players are not as skilled as they are. The highest level thinkers may come to the conclusion that the game takes into account many different levels of strategic thinkers and their actions are based upon the aspects of their complex environment. Their higher forms of action may appear irrational to lower level players only because they can't understand them.

Assume that a game has two players with defined rules. Complexity of thinking would be limited to understanding the rules of the game and a single other player. If the game had five players with different abilities and poorly defined rules it is a safe belief to assume that each player is seeking the most advantaged position. Level-k decisions would help to identify their strategy in achieving these goals. As the game becomes more complex with more players testing the environment becomes even more important. Each low level position can test the environment before making more direct moves.

Expanding on the concepts within the paper it is important to make a distinction between irrational behavior and perceived irrational behavior. In small games with clearly defined rules the rational choices are obvious. In larger games, without restrictions, what one may see as an irrational choice may yet be a most rational choice. These choices depend on objective, environmental testing behavior, countering limited thinking of other players, or even drawing in the behavior of other players.

Strategic thinking is important as organizations seek to move from local to global marketplaces where the environment has many more options and choices. The perception of rationality is based upon the abilities of those who are doing the judging and their ability to understand the environment. As cognitive complexity rises, so does the ability of individuals to make choices where the rationality is not immediately apparent to lower level thinkers. Being open to changing movements and environmental conditions can be a successful strategic choice.

The Development of Fluidity

Strategy is a key method of navigating organizations to and through environmental changes. A paper by Tamas Meszaros provides some insight into the development of strategy over the past few decades (2012). He argues that strategy has moved from being something concrete to something more fluid. His arguments make sense in terms of the ability of executives to put forward strategies but then adjust those strategies based upon an ever changing environment.

If we think of how fluid each decade has become with an advent of technology we may find that strategy is no longer stale and concise but is more of a trajectory toward organizational goals. The paths can change and adjust as new information and new pressures become apparent. As the environment changes so does the need to change the strategies based upon developing factors.

According to Cummings, et. al. (2009) history has changed the way we view strategy:

-1960's: Strategy was seen as a thing. Decisions in the present aim the organization toward a future outcome.

- 1990's: Strategy was seen as a verb. Past practices create patterns that influence the present and future.

-Present: Strategy can be seen as an adjective or adverb. How future characteristics encourage current activities that creates paths to success.

The development of strategic thought is a result of the development of human thought processes. What was once seen as rigid is more fluid. Strategy can be seen as a future orientation based upon perception. The method of achieving the fulfillment of that perception rests on particular thoughts and actions that lead to the creation of a reality.

Planning is a precursor to strategy (Roney, 1976). Planning should take into account the various resources, cultures, abilities, market trends, and other factors in order to make reasonable predictions of outcomes. Yet these outcomes should have a focus on some achievable objective in the future. Strategy is the market approach that takes into consideration the available resources found in the planning stages.

There is no definitive strategy for obtaining needed outcomes. *"Three decades of experience with strategic planning have taught us about the need to loosen up the process of strategy making rather than trying to seal it off by arbitrary formalization."* (Mintzberg, 1994.,p. 114.). Despite strategic fluidity there are some methods such as the Delphi Method, SWOT analysis and other methods that have proven track records. It should be remembered that such systems are ways of formalizing thoughts and are not infallible nor do they apply to all situations equally.

Others have described the new strategic planning process of simply being more adaptive by nature. "*Strategic planning processes have changed substantially over the past two decades in response to the challenges of strategy formulation in turbulent and unpredictable environments. Strategic planning processes have become more decentralized, less staff driven, and more informal... permitting... greater adaptability and responsiveness to external change.*" (Grant, R., 2003.p.515). As circumstances change so does the need to ensure that new information is calculated within the strategy.

Strategy is a fluid process that is based upon previous models that have worked well. One should not be so confined to these models as to not see new information as it enters into the situation. Strategy has moved from being a centralized function to taking on a more fluid decentralization. The reason is that the environment has become more fluid and requires new cognitive skills to master. Strategy starts in the planning process and takes into account desired goals and attempts to match them with current resources and potentially successful paths to achieving those goals. Strategies should be evaluated and changed when the fluid environment deems it necessary. Such strategies should not be so fluid as to create chaos without a goal but should not be so rigid as to maintain an improper course of action.

Creativity Develops Strategic Thinking

Creativity is an important component of strategic thinking. Those who are able to imagine and think through varying scenarios are capable of predicting the end game. Research by Larson and Angus helps shed light on the process of creative learning and its association with developing critical strategies (2011). This learning can start in high school and move into the early college years and continues throughout one's life.

The development of agency is an important tool for achieving goals and ensuring the ability to move through a changing environment. Projects in young adulthood and early college can help to develop the mental faculty of seeing projects to their completion as well as thinking creatively about solving problems. Education should have a level of creative faculty to develop these skills to match concrete content learning.

Agency skills also develop the ability to have executive control over one's own thoughts, learn new cognitive tools, develop creative problem solving, learn the action skills to achieve goals and move into higher order thinking. These skills and abilities further create a platform for strategic thinking. Without the ability to think creatively, it is doubtful that new methods and paths will develop.

Programs often use the "arc of work" approach which includes the concepts of planning, monitoring, adjusting existing plans and receiving feedback. When projects span of a period of weeks and months it requires students to be reflective of their creative process. When the situation changes the students can find ways of adapting to those changes. It is this thinking about and reflection on methods that helps students find new ways to complete their projects in meaningful ways.

When people are engaged in projects and own the results they invest themselves into the process more deeply. It is an investment that helps create higher order thinking and strategic planning. The creation of a long-term project helps to connect the many different work methods and strategies students use to navigate their environment. It helps solidify successful methods from unsuccessful ones. They are likely to use these approaches later in their working life.

The researchers used 11 different programs to assess the results of the creative process. They worked back into the creative process and conducted in-depth research to assess how such projects foster creative strategic thinking. A few years later, they interviewed the participants again to create a longitudinal approach. They looked at artistic programs, social activism, media arts, political action, and leadership programs. An in-depth review of plans, thought processes, and perceptions were particularly important.

The participants reported that they learned how to mobilize their efforts and regulate their time. They gained the long-term perspective to that allowed them to create strategies to complete their projects. Their plans were broken down into action steps. Steps are seen as sequential actions that lead to project completion. Most remarkably, participants learned that strategic thinking requires the ability to adjust with changing circumstances, understand how others respond, think through the alternatives, and have backup plans.

The greatest advantage is that students were able to think through how human systems operate and what cognitive models others use to respond to their various actions. In addition, they were able to transfer the skills learned to other areas in life including prediction of events and determining alternative actions. Strong strategy includes all of the functions related to projecting outcomes; determine alternative strategies, understanding the tasks, and a greater theoretical understanding of the environment.

The report connects the concepts of creative thinking and analytical analysis to determine the potential scenarios. The authors come to a definition of strategic thinking as '*Use of advanced executive skills to anticipate possible scenarios in the steps to achieving goals and to formulate flexible courses of action that take these possibilities into account.*'' Strategy is a process of first envisioning the possibilities and then systematically thinking through the likely outcomes of results. It is both a freethinking and analytical process where possibilities are explored and the most likely ones chosen. The creative mind is able to adjust its processes when the environment calls for such changes.

Scientific Learning Fosters Decision-Making

Socio-scientific discussions are rarely specific enough to give a concrete answer. The complexity of making determinations in this field helps in highlighting which methods of strategic decision-making people are using. Research by Eggert & Bogeholz delves into the complex decision-making process students use to make socio-scientific decisions based upon competing information and ambiguous direction (1994). Their results show that scientific thinking improves complexity of thought and strategy making.

The process of making decisions that border between scientific research and sociological concepts is difficult. In scientific research it is necessary to answer both ambiguous and specific questions like the potential societal benefits of research or the exact measurements used in instrumentation. It is hard for people to make cognitive models that can handle such information effectively.

Understanding science requires the ability to look at data, be open to new data, and understand its implications on people. It is a higher skill set that not everyone can develop and those who do have spent years learning. It uses analytical thinking, creativity, systematic approaches, and sociological perspectives all meshed together to come to conclusions.

Science can enhance skills in argumentation, decision-making, and problem-solving. Strategy can be developed when people learn about trade-offs which is seen as the ability to weigh and balance certain factors. Where a loss occurs in one set of options there can be gain in another set of options. Most people are limited to only a few factors and simply cut off the rest. As intelligence and knowledge increases more factors can be incorporated into the systematic thinking process without having to automatically limit oneself to a few simple possibilities.

In science it is possible to make decisions on key pieces of data. Each one has their own weight of influence. To come to better conclusions a level of meta-reflection on the decision making process is necessary to ensure that thinking patterns are appropriate and not biasing the outcome. To do this well requires the integration of multiple pieces of information, seeing how they interact, determining trade-offs of different factors, and reflecting on the whole process.

Complexity of thinking ranges from spontaneous thinking with no reflection to higher levels of tradeoffs with meta-reflection. Intermediate thinkers use both cut offs and tradeoffs with some level of reflection on the thinking process. The highest level scientific thinkers use tradeoffs with relative weighting to think through possibilities. The far majority of people use cut-offs because it is easier to work with limited data that don't consider the options.

The researchers Eggert & Bogeholz used the Rasch partial credit model to determine the competencies German science students were using to make decisions. A total of 436 students were engaged within the study and assessed based upon their decision-making skills. Their work helps highlight that even with a scientific education the skill can be increased but is not developed by everyone.

The results showed that science education raised non-compensatory decision-making strategies to mixed strategies and then to tradeoff strategies as people developed. Participants had difficulty weighing many different criteria to make appropriate decisions. Meta-reflection changed thinking from a content specific analysis to a strategic analysis that is based on an analysis of multiple options.

The majority of participants used the cut off method that focused on looking at a single or few aspects of the overall problem. They had difficulty weighing and balancing a greater amounts of information, points, and criteria to get a more concrete picture. As a person's education rises from six to twelve years their ability to manage more pieces of information grew tremendously.

The cognitive structure and complexity of thought are important aspects of making decisions and developing a strategy. It is a skill that increases as one spends more time in school or learning about science. Generally, the more one is capable of balancing multiple pieces of information the more able they are to build progressive strategies that achieve goals. Seeing information through varying possibilities and weighing and balancing the likelihood of each outcome is a higher order skill. Quickly discarding options without thorough analysis limits how well one can respond to environmental challenges. The report helps to show how leaders decision-making ability can be enhanced by focusing on evidence based strategic management and then reflecting on those decisions to ensure they are accurate.

Feedback Loops Create Strategy

In strategy, it is necessary to develop not only the action but also the feedback loop to ensure effectiveness. Research by Newell, et. al (2013) using dice rolls indicates that top-down strategies are quickly developed while the changing of poor strategic choices through bottom-up discoveries in feedback develop slower. It helps decision makers understand they may be quick to accept optimizing strategies but slow in adjusting course once those strategies are enacted. An unyielding strategy could potentially lead to poor results.

People often use probability matching when determining a strategy which is based on the probability of outcome. For example, if people believe they will have a payoff 70% of the time they are likely to choose that option 70% of the time even it could be chosen 100% of the time for more effectiveness. Optimization requires the ability to understand the factors within the game.

When people are provided feedback of outcomes it is believed they would optimize at a greater level than those who did not receive feedback. It is also believed that optimization for maximum results are ingrained into strategic decision making with feedback being a key factor that fosters effective behavior. Likewise, it is also logical that people should be open to feedback for improvement.

When participants were provided with hints, they were much more likely to find an optimizing strategy. They did this by focusing on the payoffs of each dice role. Even when information is available without hints a large portion of people were unable to come to an awareness of a proper strategy. Strategy is then seen as a function of awareness of information within the environment and the implications of that information.

The researchers Newell, et. al (2011) used two dice games with 7 greens and 3 red sides. Some participants were provided with hints while others were not. Likewise, some were provided with feedback while others were not. They designed the games to ensure that both the maximization and the matching strategies were available as potential choices to determine what method participants used.

Despite having all of the information available from the beginning of the game, it was the feedback with a hint that helped participants maximizes their strategies. A majority of participants didn't appear to make meaning from the feedback information without a hint. Participants that did formulate strategies sought and tested new strategies over subsequent trials. A large percentage of participants thought of a quick strategy and used it throughout the game without changing their behavior. A small group of individuals were found with superior cognitive abilities that optimized their strategies without feedback or hints.

The study does relate to business strategy development. Executives may use a particular strategy and continue with that strategy (top down) and ignore feedback (bottom up) that would help them adjust and improve their strategy. These strategic choices are often made in the earliest part of the game before information is readily available making them often inaccurate. This can lead to disastrous results when an environmental scan and feedback loop are not included to ensure direction adjusts to increase strategic accuracy. Even worse, if a poor strategy is used to its natural conclusion it may be far off of the mark. A small percentage of people may be able to look at the factors involved, and develop their own strategies and have the cognitive flexibility to continue the adjustment of their approaches as information becomes available. Openness to information equates to success in successful strategy management.

The Social Context and Social Cognition of Strategy Formation

Strategy is not only the logical components of actions that lead to goal achievement. True strategy has significant social aspects based within the cognitive understanding of workers, stakeholders, and even customers. A paper by Vallaster and Muehlbacher (2012) outlines the social representations inherent within strategy formation and its social context of development.

They argue that a large part of strategy formation is social and must be enacted in a social environment.

Strategic success must take into account actions, interactions, and negotiations of multiple actors. Each person realizes the strategy through his or her own vantage point and previous practices. Strategy must fit within others mental framework in order to be successful and fully implemented throughout an organization.

Strategizing takes includes 1.) narratives, 2.) actors personal interests, 3.) organizational design, culture and past practices, and 4.) market factors. Strategic development should take into account the multiple factors and their potential weight in order to be successful and navigate the social environment.

Individual context-dependent interpretations influence the way in which people make decisions. As new information is presented it changes past schemata to that which is in transition and finally to new schemata. Thus, each strategy is situational dependent on the understandings of those involved in its formation and those who are going to carry it out.

Strategy is also dependent on the internal workings and actors of an organization. Through the process of strategic development a company's practices and cultural perceptions will affect a strategies fulfillment. In other words, the way in which people think will influence how they see the strategy and its potential benefits to themselves.

As most strategies seek to find competitive advantages, the market and various outside stakeholders will create pressure on the strategy and influence its perception. As the human mind considers the effectiveness of potential strategies these external factors, will act in judgment and will naturally create pressures. Poor strategy that does not consider the external structure and pressures is likely to fail.

The way in which society views and interacts with itself will influence strategy through social representations. Social representations are 1.) complex formations of knowledge that comes from social discourse, and 2.) socio-cognitive processes that come from that discourse. As something new enters into society's awareness there is a communication process that comes to define it. In other words, society settles on meaning and then projects that meaning.

Strategies consist of core and peripheral elements. Core strategies are seen as logical and have shared cognitions based within the common perspectives of the participants (i.e. customer oriented service as a strategy). According to the authors, the actor must believe in their realities and put those forward to others but should also be willing to bend these understandings to create shared realities among a group of people.

Each person within the strategy will have to make personal meaning from it. Therefore, each participant has sub-strategies related to their place within the strategy based upon their memories and understandings (Barsalou, 1999). They use their past experiences to find meaning within the strategy.

The peripheral aspects of the strategies include those who are not directly related to the strategy formation but may be impacted by it. For example, customers who have needs of quality and experience should have their information considered as this improves upon the strategies effectiveness. Without understanding the impact on the environment or others, it is doubtful such strategies will be fully effective.

The authors bring forward the concept that the context strategy formation is as much social as it is logical. Logic is the center but the social aspects are the periphery. All strategic decisions must take into account the impact and perceptions of others. When stakeholders cannot make meaning or formulate a social connection to the strategy, it is unlikely to be fruitful.

The authors dance around the concept of social projection. Projection is a concept brought forward by Freud to describe how one unconsciously projects their traits onto another. Social projection in strategy is the idea that strategy is built from the inner and outer understandings of the maker(s) and can be projected forth from a group. For example, a company that is losing their financial and competitive position may rally their executives to formulate a strategy. Once that strategy has been created, it can be projected onto others within the organization in the attempt to foster action that fulfills the strategy. That strategy is a direct result of how the decision makers think and can lead to social behaviors of others that make it a reality.

Aligning the Organization to Environmental Demands

Corporate competitiveness is a process that requires continually adjustment to the market to increase efficiency and effectiveness. A paper by Bhattachariya and Gibbons (1996), discusses in further depth how this environmental alignment can be achieved. By ensuring organizations are structured in a way that improves competitiveness, they can also help secure a place in the global economy.

Greater internationalization, consumer choice, fragmented markets, and short product cycles are some of the challenges organizations face. Companies increasingly are forced to change with environmental demands and are attempting to meet these demands through transformation of their structures. A proper transformation should align the organization and everything within it to corporate strategies that match the market environment.

Two primary constraints influence businesses, which include the external environment and a level of performance that is sufficient to deal with that environment. To find the balance means one must find a strategy that positions the organization into a competitive stance. That strategy is a way to achieve an objective; it is a path to a goal.

The external environment is the environment, which the organization is currently working. It may be global in nature, could include the local labor market, or focus on regulatory environments. It is all of the pressures and factors found through a proper environmental scan. The performance level of the organization should be able to compete effectively in that market if there is to be success.

The entire structure should be aligned to the environmental needs. This requires the ability to ensure processes and procedures are fulfilling the organizations functions. It is these processes and procedures do not fulfill a competitive need and alignment to the market then it is necessary to reduce them as waste.

Success can come through creating number of adjustments within the layers of structure and the alignment of related processes. This includes the strategy, the business unit strategies, the functional strategies, processes, and competencies/capabilities. The business unit strategies take into consideration actual functional aspects of the firm. This includes marketing, financial, purchasing, and manufacturing, etc…

Each strategy should focus on what the organization does well. If innovation is a core competency, all processes and procedures should align to the environment in a way that further enhances these competencies. For example, innovation would require a level of experimentation, collaboration, flatter organizational structure, and open-minded management, and constant communication. The organization should seek to develop processes and procedures that enhance this innovation to compete in an environment with lower product cycle times and competitive offerings.

The author does not discuss cognitive processes. As processes and procedures are learned employees naturally begin to change the way they think about proper work functions. The longer such processes and procedures are used the more they become embedded within the organizational culture and the mindset of the employees. To have a truly transformational change requires the changing of thoughts and behavior.

It is possible to make conclusions about environmental alignment as a process:

-Adjusting organizational strategy to match environmental demands.

-Adjusting business unit (departmental) strategies to match organizational strategies.

-Create functional strategies that are in alignment with the departmental and corporate strategies.

-Adjust processes to fulfill the functional strategies, departmental strategies and corporate strategies.

-Encourage new employee cognitive and behavioral strategies that match the needs of the processes, functional strategies, departmental strategies, business unit strategies and organizational strategies.

Conclusion

Strategy formation is a creative, social and analytical process that seeks to find appropriate paths that meet market needs. All strategies should take into account the environmental demands of the market and seek to align the organization to compete more effectively on the market. To do this well requires the ability to understand the market through systematic testing and then formulate actions that will achieve the greatest level of social and financial returns.

Companies align themselves to the market needs. These needs are often seen through multiple perspectives such as customer preferences, market trends, economic development, culture, legislation, and anything else that can have an impact on the company. The more vantage points considered the more accurate the environmental assessment. A thorough environmental scan with analysis will be needed to meet this market need.

Strategy is a cognitive process based within the perspectives of decision-makers and how they perceive the world. It is limited by the thought processes of those involved as well as information available. If executives are only capable of processing information in a cut-off approach they are likely to miss important environmental cues and make incorrect strategy assumptions.

After a strategy has been formulized it is projected throughout the organization. Each employee must make meaning out of this strategy and ultimately agree with the approach. Employees will use sub-strategies that will benefit themselves in the process before deciding to further or resist the strategy. Each employee will make that decision on their own regardless of the approach and manner in which it is outlined.

As decision-makers are prone to finding a quick strategy, based upon their past experiences, without actually understanding cues and information from the environment there is a strong likelihood that an inflexible strategy will result in ineffective results. All strategies should be open to new information found in the environment as well as changing circumstances. These strategies should change when the trends of the market significantly change.

Each component of the organization ultimately should align to the basic principles of the strategy to create efficiency. The employee tasks, procedures, policies, financing, recruitment, products, marketing, etc. should all be in alignment with the overriding strategy. This will eventual create cognitive processes within employees that seek to obtain gain within the organization. It is those cognitive processes that create sustainability and synergy of action.

After a strategy has been fully implemented it is necessary to develop feedback loops. These loops help executives collect and make meaning of information obtained from the results of the implemented strategies. When the environment changes the feedback loops should be adequate enough to ensure that decision-makers are made aware and can readjust their strategies for more effectiveness when necessary.

Steps to Strategy Development:

1.) Research and understand the market and current abilities of the organization.

2.) Determine higher level goals and objectives to ensure they are relevant and valuable to customers and employees.

3.) Determine the sub-department strategies that help align their activities to the higher level goals.

4.) Develop an implementation plan that systematically adjusts the entire organization to meet these goals and objectives.

4.) Review the strategy, seek multiple vantage points, and understand how one's personal attributes influence the strategy.

5.) Project the strategy both socially and systematically throughout the organization.

6.) Review implementation to ensure it has moved to specific actions and expectations of employees. Make sure that resources and abilities of the organization are aligned. Determine time frames and goals for the implementation of new strategies.

7.) Develop feedback loops both internally and within the market to determine if the strategy needs to be readjusted. Review and meet to determine if strategic adjustments are necessary.

References

Barsalou, L. W. (1999): Perceptional Symbol Systems. *Behavioral and Brain Science, 22* (1999).

Bhattacharya, A. & Gibbons, A. (1996). Strategy formulation: focusing on core competencies and processes. *Business Change & Re-engineering, 3* (1).

Crawford, V., et. al. (2013) Structural models of nonequilibrium strategic thinking: theory, evidence and applications. *Journal of Economic Literature, 51* (1).

Cummings, S. & Daellenbach, U. (2009). A guide to the future of strategy? *The history of long-range planning, 42.*

Effert, S. & Bogeholz, S. (2010). Student's use of decision-making strategies with regard to socioscientific issues: an application of Rasch partial credit model. *Science Education, 94* (2)

El Namaki, S. (2013). Strategic thinking for turbulent times. *Ivey Business Journal, 77* (4).

Grant R. (2003): Strategic planning in a turbulent environment: Evidence from the Oil and Gas Majors, *Strategic Management Journal, 24.*

Larson, R. & Angus, R. (2011). Adolescents' development of skills for agency in youth programs: learning to think strategically. *Child Development, 82* (1).

Meszaros, T. (2012). Traditional and new elements in strategic thinking. International Journal of Management, 14 (1).

Mintzberg, H. (1994). *The Rise and Fall of Strategic Planning.* Prentice Hall, Englewood Cliffs,N.J.

Newell, B, et. al. (2013). Probability matching in risky choice: the interplay of feedback and

    strategy availability. *Memory and Cognition, 41* (3).

Pop, Z. & Borza, A. (2013). Summarizing the crucial steps of the strategic management process

    through the eyes of Romanian managers of SMES. Review *of Economic Studies &*

    Research Virgil Madgearu, 6 (1).

Roney, C. (1976). The two purposes of business planning. *Managerial Planning*

1976/Nov.-Dec.

Schaefer, et. al. (2013). Communicative versus strategic rationality: Haberman's theory of

    communicative action and the social brain. *PloS One, 29* (5).

Vallaster, C. and Muehlbacher, H. (2012). Strategy formation as social representation:

    understanding the influence of contexts on strategy formation.

    Betriebswirtschaft/Business Administration Review, 72 (5).

Developing Leadership Communications

"The most important thing in communication is hearing what isn't said."

-Peter Drucker

Developing Strong Communications

Communication is a fundamental function of leadership and leads to eminence in influence. Leadership exists within social networks and is reliant upon those networks for both information as well as social support. As technology develops, new methods of communication are used to expand messages to reach more people than was possible only a few decades ago. The use of proper face-to-face communication and online communication influences the overall effectiveness of spreading messages to the greatest amount of people with highest level of social impact. The effective use of marketing channels improves upon the overall ability of people to spread their messages and influence cognitive processes of those who receive the information and make meaning from it.

Regardless of the channels used, the general mechanics of proper communication stay the same. As leaders learn to communicate effectively they are encouraging the development of follower's cognitive models through the incorporation of new information. A premise of strong leadership is to help people see new perspectives and opportunities that were once mentally closed to them. The use of communication is centered on influence through raising awareness that offers proper paths for engagement and higher levels of group involvement.

Throughout history, we have seen some great leaders come and many go but most are remembered only for a short time. Those that make their place in history are the ones who can rally people to a cause based upon the charisma of their communication styles and the far reaching implications of their messages. Whether one is the leader of a public body of people, or an executive in a business, the overall components of developing strong communication stay the same. The question of how a leader creates motivation through new cognitive understandings is a difficult one to answer.

Verbal and Non-Verbal Communication

Spoken language is the medium that allows us to express ourselves and obtain information from our social group. Those who communicate well are likely to find additional success that poor communicators are unlikely to realize. A paper by Binod Mishra (2009) helps to define how both verbal and non-verbal components of language interact to create higher levels of communicative skill.

He argues that social media interferes with our ability to communicate while writing reports and papers improve upon this ability. Social media such as texting might be more like "ttyl" or "brb". The medium of cell phones limits full expression without significant effort and cost to the user in terms of contracts. Report writing, as seen in college, helps to encourage higher levels of expression. However, few things compare to the verbal skills and non-verbal cues we use when communicating with others in a face-to-face or video format.

Verbal Skills: Verbal skills are the vocal messages we send to others. They can be figurative or literal. How loud we speak, the type of voice, pitch and pronunciation say something about us as a person as well as the message we are sharing. Most of us consciously focus on the verbal words but subconsciously pick up the non-verbal cues. Together they create the total message.

Voice: This is the way in which we utilize our voice to give hints about our nature and attitude.

Volume: People should be knowledgeable enough to lower or raise one's voice based upon the audience and room acoustics.

Pitch: Average rate of words between 120 and 175 words per minute.

Pronunciation: The ability and skill to say the words correctly.

Non-Verbal Cues:

Sigmund Freud once said, "*He who has eyes to see and ears to hear can convince that no mortal can keep a secret. If his lips are silent, he chats with his finger tips, betrayal oozes out of him at every pore.*" The way in which we use our body reveals the other true meanings of our messages. When we align our body with our messages we make a more trustworthy communication style that motivates people to believe and act on the information.

Facial Expression: The face creates honest language based within our biological development. Feelings like pain, annoyance, and joy are common. The face also shows confusion, mischief, and many other thought processes.

Eyes: The eyes are the "windows of our soul" and expresses truthfulness, intimacy, concern naughtiness, joy, surprise, curiosity, affection and love. Make eye contact with the target of your conversation.

Body Movements: Gestures and postures also contribute to communication even when the speaker doesn't know it.

Silence and Pauses: Using pauses and silence can emphasis meanings and interest.

Verbal and non-verbal communication works together to create clear channels of information transference. People are often aware of the verbal skills but are less able to understand the non-verbal communications. These subtle impressions further define the information that is transferred from one person to the next. Being aware of these subtle cues improves upon your decoding of information but also you to pick up on other messages it contains.

Language Semantics

Semantics is a concept that helps define a word within the context of other words. It is often derived from word selection and connotation. Semantics can come from multiple forms of subtle meaning to create impressions in the listener's mind. Those who can master semantics can create higher forms of communicative ability and influence. From sales opportunities to leadership semantics has a huge impact on how each of the individual parts of a message creates a whole understanding of that message.

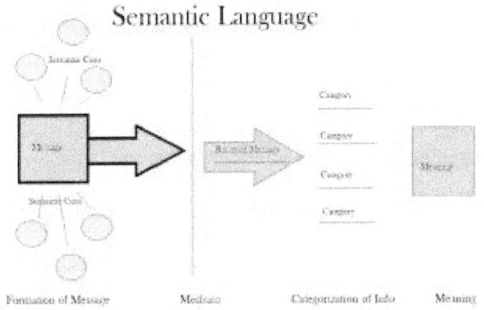

Semantics can take information from multiple sources such as tone, word choice, word order, tone, facial expressions (paralanguage), and other subtle impressions that help define the full message. When used in combination the clarity of language is enhanced due to its focus of symbolism to create a single shared meaning both in part and together. To understand how they work together can create a powerful message.

Each sentence and word is associated with those around it and within the context of the environment. The way in which people make connections between this information can be argued as either an inborn part of natural language or developed throughout cultural vantage points. Many researchers are still unsure of which philosophical approach to take. However, they do agree that the connection of words to their meaning occurs through cognitive abilities and is associated with higher thought.

Research helps show how semantic enhancement of language is associated with the personal abilities of individuals. For example, those who are in tune with music are also more capable in semantic usage (Bidelman, et. al, 2013). This is associated with their higher perceptual understanding of tones and the ability to discern between subtleties. A large body of research associates artistic endeavors with sensitivity to environmental information.

Strong communication and use of pitch can enhance presentation skills and overall sales. Sales departments that are strong on their use of semantics are likely to be more effective in their transference of information that allows the buyer to come to their own conclusions. People can often judge the meaning behind the words, attitude, tone, and sincerity of message (Gitomer, 2013). This creates higher levels of verbal continuity which can translate into dollars.

The use of semantics can also help listeners created categories in their minds making the message much easier to follow. Semantics usage contributes to perception and cognition when they lead to the proper categorization of information and create spatial understandings (Choi & Hattrup, 2012). Those speakers who use semantics to enhance their messages can also create categorization and clarity within the minds of listeners.

Semantics is a fundamental aspect of natural language. Research conducted on motion verbs in 100 languages found similarities between words of related meanings (Walchli &

Cysouw, 2012). Similarities of meanings exist in multiple languages and create a more basic form of semantic identity. This identity indicates that semantics is more basic than abstract thought and is part of a fundamental building block.

Semantic language usage enhances the power of leaders to communicate their message with clarity by creating categories in the minds of readers. It also allows the ability to influence actions and behaviors of others who use these messages to cue expectations and behaviors. Even though semantic language is an inherent part of communicating it is often outside of the average person's awareness. Awareness does not mean that they are not collecting these cues subconsciously to make meaning and decisions. It could be argued that unconscious use of semantic language may be more powerful than its conscious use. Sales, executives, and public speakers would do well to learn how semantic information influences their communication abilities.

Paralanguage

Paralanguage is related to the use of subtle messages that includes tone, prosody, intonation, tempo, syllable emphasis, and other hints that create additional meaning beyond the words themselves. Knowing and understanding how paralanguage influences clarity can help in creating more effective

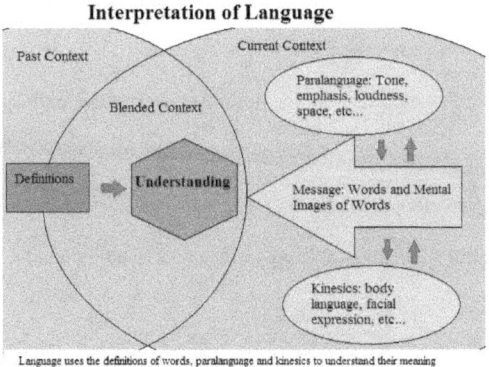

Interpretation of Language

Language uses the definitions of words, paralanguage and kinesics to understand their meaning within the current and past context.

conversation in the workplace. Managers who are capable of creating higher levels of congruency between the words they use and the paralanguage associated with those words can increase their communication effectiveness and organizational influence.

Most information comes from non-verbal aspects of communication and alignment between these two concepts creates congruence. A study of university lecturers helped identify that those who used appropriate pitch, loudness, variability, pauses, and fluency increased audience satisfaction (Md Zani, et. al, 2011). The audience paid more attention and were more focused on the concepts. This helps ensure that the messages not only came across well but were also received by members of the audience.

If the use of paralanguage can benefit the quality of communication in a public forum it can also benefit management and employee relationships. As employees seek to understand expectations, directions, and practical information they will listen beyond the words into paralanguage to determine both intent and hidden meaning. This intent, whether positive or negative, will help ensure the truthfulness of the message.

In many cases employees are not consciously aware of these messages and intuitively prescribe them to the words being spoken. The use of paralanguage is a system that develops within a cultural heritage to further expand the language capabilities between members (Wang De-hue, 2007). Because we are raised within a particular culture we may have some difficulty interpreting the meaning of messages from other cultures. The more we associate with other cultures the more able we are to understand their subtle messages.

We begin to become aware of that language at a young age in the same way that we become aware of social context. At the age of six children are still more likely to judge the actual words versus the subtle differences in paralanguage (Morton & Trehub 2001). Yet by the time they become adults they are much more astute at this overall judgment between spoken language and its subtle paralanguage.

To create congruence of language also creates clarity in the message as well as its perceived honesty. For many managers it is about being aware of such language and its potential impact on employees that will help them create stronger relationships with employees as well as more effectiveness within their management style. It is through continuous practice that managers can improve both the giving as well as the reception of such messages.

Organizations should consider a level of training in language usage as it pertains to the workplace. A number of studies have indicated that both written and verbal communication skills are important factors of success in the workplace. Employee resistance, misinterpretation, wasted employee effort, conflict, and general labor relations are all associated with the proper use of language. The concept becomes even more important as leaders grow in influence and power. It is difficult for them to clearly articulate their strategic visions if they are inadvertently giving off mixed signals that are interpreted differently by different sectors of society.

Practical Use of Communication in Negotiations

The world of negotiations requires subtle use of verbal and body language that effectively meets objectives. According to a paper by Yuxian Zhang (2013) negotiations is a process of coming to mutual benefit and reducing borders between sides. What we say and how we say it can impact the success of getting people to understand our point of view. Negotiations are all about sharing perspective and understanding each other's needs.

Language is the primary method of negotiating in business. A famous negotiator by the name of Cohen Herbert argues that negotiation is not about *"winning by defeating the other party, but winning by getting what both parties want"*. This is not possible if the language does not draw people into a shared perspective and instead creates mental chasms that cannot be crossed.

Robin Lakoff argues that there are three main principles in social linguistics that help to create politeness and shared perspective that are beneficial in negotiations:

-Don't impost your beliefs on or rewrite the affairs of others.

-Provide options and choices and let others decide what to do.

-Treat each other with fairness and respect to create equality in the relationship.

The key is to understand others and ensure they understand you. It is possible to do so when the negotiation environment is not testy or confrontational which closes down people's openness to the perspective of others. To transfer your information effectively requires the use of verbal and non-verbal cues.

Verbal cues are often rooted in our word choices and verbs. Saying things like "you must" or "you are" keep the finger pointed in the other direction while works like "we are" or "we should consider" draw both sides into a shared perspective. Non-verbal cues are the facial expressions, clothing, environment, and body language that contribute to the perceived truthfulness and intent of other party.

The impressions may be as subtle as a simple look or a brief impression. According to a Spanish philosopher by the name of Autauga, *"the speaker's eyes can tell you their inner world"*. When people are trying to interpret a message, they often look for clues even though they may not be wholly aware of them on a conscious level. Each impression they receive influences the meaning of the total message.

Moving beyond this paper there is an important concept of perspective taking that makes its way throughout the entire negotiation process. If a person cannot mentally reverse themselves and see the world through the opposing side's view they will not be able to find the right words that help them come to the same conclusions. It is nearly impossible without the use of pure force to come to a mutual understanding if there is no ability to walk in another person's moccasins.

Becoming an Influencer

Improving communication skills and influencing others is important for potential success in leadership and business management. A paper by Johnson and Young (2012) discusses the concepts of influencing others to achieve personal and professional objectives. Their advice appears to be practical in the sense that it continues to expand social networks by creating more adherents. It also takes into account the natural resistance people display and how to overcome some of the concerns.

Most people tune out a significant amount of daily conversation and the majority of information is lost from one day to the next. To attract someone's interests it is sometimes necessary to do or ask something interesting. In sales they may call this "making the pitch" but in daily conversation it is more of "tuning in" to potential engagement.

Most people are receptive to things that help them achieve their personal goals. Explaining concepts through their vantage point and the potential benefits of certain actions helps them to visualize the possibilities. Encouraging others to engage a solution is influence at its most fundamental state.

Before one can properly influence others they need to be asking the right questions. This is a process of brainstorming and thinking about all of the alternatives. Asking the right questions can prompt other people to start thinking about the answers and if their answers logically lead to your conclusions you are likely to find support. People willingly engage solutions when they come to cognitive agreement.

Each organization comes with other influencers and connecting them together creates systematic impact. Communicating with opinion leaders and power brokers creates the ability to render converts to a cause and then move those ideas throughout an organization. The more people who hear, understand, and pass on the concepts the more influence created.

People want to quantify the concepts for mental consumption. They want to envision, touch, taste and see the ideas. Speaking in terms of tangibles helps people understand and create a mental framework that solidifies the concepts. This allows them to formalize, ponder, and finally conclude with their agreement.

People want to understand your message. It is beneficial to use the language of your audience. This means using the terms, vocabulary, education level and at times even the slang others use. Helping people understand the message means speaking in a way that allows for easy connection to the concepts.

It is beneficial to work in a group and allow multiple vantage points and perspectives to make their way into the solutions. Doing so will afford greater allies in your quest. People have varying perspectives and these perspectives can be used to help ensure that concepts make sense to the largest amount of people.

Developing better presentations with graphics, charts, and content helps people solidify the information. Just like in sales, a great presentation can provide for higher levels of understanding. It can draw interest and put things in a tangible form.

Don't believe that you are infallible. Continue learning from your mistakes to improve upon your influencing abilities. Some things work well while others do not. If you continue to learn you are likely to improve over time and create higher abilities.

The report doesn't talk about truth but it should be included as an influencing argument. People don't want someone to "pull the wool over their eyes" or "blow smoke" and will be naturally resistant to those who have an unyielding agenda. Rightly so, as an over demanding agenda means they have not evaluated the alternatives and their concerns are limited to their own needs. People want to hear the strengths and potential pitfalls so that they can understand the credibility of the speaker. Those who think they know all the answers usually don't.

Multiple Forms of Media Impact Our Social Understandings

Communication is seen as a process of information transference from one person to another. Few think about the cognitive models that develop from information transference and how different communication channels influence meaning. Dennis, et. al. (2008) discusses the nature of information conveyance and convergence when dealing with groups and how media synchronicity impacts meaning making among recipients.

Media richness theory indicates that task performance will improve when task information are matched to the medium's information richness. Difficult tasks require more information when compared to simple tasks while less rich media are better suited to tasks that require less information. The media used to transfer information should be based on the type of task that needs to be accomplished.

For example, someone who wants to complete a simple task such as changing a wiper blade on a car will need few instructions to successfully complete this task. Changing a car transmission may require multiple forms of written instructions and videos to successful complete this task. The more difficult the task, the more media synchronicity is useful. Information should be displayed in a step-by-step process.

In communication we prepare information, transfer it through a medium, and others will process this information into their mental models. Different people obtain varying levels of information from media and process that information according to how their particular mental models work. Two people can see the same thing but each will notice the information that fits within their understanding while selectively ignoring information that does not fit within their personal models.

In groups, the meaning of information is based more in the interactive interpretation of multiple persons. Meaning requires a level of negotiation among members that are engaged in tasks. Meaning is subjective depending on the cognitive models others are using. Each group will come to their own slightly different interpretation of the information.

When transmitting information to groups it is important to understand the processes of conveyance and convergence. Conveyance processes provide transmission of diversity of new information that allows individuals to create revised mental models of situations. Convergence processes is the way in which people interpret and make models out of the information to come to mutually agreed upon understandings. We can see this as receiving information, building models of that information, and then coming to a shared understanding of that information.

It is possible to see this in an example. The latest gizmo makes its way on the market. The type of spokes models, celebrities, music, and impressions provided through the media make their way into everyday conversations. Each interpretation adds to the collective development of a fad product. When the product becomes old people will leave it for something new. That is the nature of fads and hype which is socially constructed concepts of "coolness" that change over time.

The researchers found that when individuals have experience with tasks and each other they have fewer convergence processes and less need for media synchronicity. In other words, they are familiar with each other's cognitive processes and a small amount of information is enough for them to come to a shared understanding (i.e. a tight group of teenagers who like a product). When individuals have little experience with each other or the tasks it is beneficial to use multiple rich forms of media to transfer needed information.

The study helps highlight how we use media and information to build cognitive models. When tasks are unfamiliar it is beneficial to use multiple forms of rich media to help us build new models (i.e. learning) and come to a social understanding of those models. Once the models are built, lower forms of media are enough to transfer information. Thus, understanding is based on cognitive models and they are individually constructed and then negotiated against others cognitive models to come to a mutual understanding. Therefore, understanding is a social construction process fostered by the information we receive from our environment and multiple forms of media (i.e. phone, Internet, face-to-face, music, television, You Tube, etc…) that help us make sense out of it.

Biology and Personality Influences Communication Styles

The authors Waldherr and Muck (2011) discuss how biology and personality contribute to communication behavior. They advocate embedding language into the Five-Factor Theory to better assess language as a characteristic adaptation to personality. The arguments put forward in their literary research lean more heavily on personality as a key factor that has two major running themes.

Communication is a circular process as each of the actors is both the communicator and the recipient at various times during a discussion (Schramm, 1954). Each person encodes, interprets and decodes messages differently making the communication process unique. Most of this process is internal to the individual and cannot be easily evaluated. Focusing on verbal, non-verbal and para-verbal language cues can help in evaluating communication patterns.

Communication is seen as a reoccurring behavioral pattern that is personality based. It is expressed in varying ways in different situations to achieve directed goals. How one communicates in one situation or in the next will have similar deeply embedded goals and expressive styles even though the terms, words, and mannerisms may be situational.

Communication behavior can be seen as "*the way one verbally or para-verbally interacts to signal how literal meaning should be taken, interpreted, filtered, or understood*" (Norton, 1978, p. 99). It is viewed as a stable pattern of behavior that stays relatively consistent across varying situations. It is commonly believed that the two major themes of assertiveness and responsiveness exist across all communicative behavior (Burgoon and Hale, 1987)

Personality and communication can also be integrally tied together. Communication is personality driven and is based within a person's biology (Beatty and McCroskey, 1998). Individuals are predetermined to communicate in certain manners based upon their genetic makeup expressed within the environment. How a person communicates and whether or not a person communicates is rooted in their personality development.

Behavior and personality often mesh within the Five-Factor Theory of Neuroticism, Extraversion, Openness, Agreeableness, and Conscientiousness (McCrae and Costa, 1996). The biology of a person predisposes them to certain types of traits that mix with their personality and are expressed in certain ways that are influenced by situational factors. These situational factors are dependent on culture, education, experience, and other life influences.

A person's can also influence communication through a self-construct. This construct is dependent on how a person views themselves in terms of being independent or interrelated to others (Markus and Kitayama, 1991). Self-construct is how a person views themselves in relation to others based upon values, beliefs, manners, skills, and a whole host of other issues. When self-constructs change it creates natural changes in communicative patterns.

The authors believe that it is important to define communication as personality rooted in the Five-Factor Theory. They also believe that communication follows two general patterns of assertiveness or responsiveness. Assertiveness is the desire to dominate others while responsiveness is more closely akin to love and interrelatedness. These two themes make their way throughout the varying learned communication skills people develop over time.

The implications of the study suggest that learned skills and experiences enhance an employee's communication skills. The patterns of communication will remain relatively the same but the complexity by which they express themselves will grow and develop over time. Business students should learn proper communication skills in order to fully express themselves in appropriate ways to others within the workplace. The learned skills can influence everything from workplace conflict to customer service and could have an impact on the bottom line. This is why it is important to hire for personality and train for skills.

Online and Offline Social Network Channels

Do your social networks impact your success? Xiaojung and Vekatesh (2013) discuss research on how important physical and online social networks are to job performance. Direct physical, direct online, and indirect online are sources of information that impact the process of decision-making and connecting to resources. Their research helps identify how online and offline communication channels can work together to enhance job performance.

It is first beneficial to define what a social network is. *"A social network is a specific set of linkages among a defined set of persons, with the additional property that the characteristics of these linkages as a whole may be used to interpret the social behavior of the persons involved"* (Mitchell, 1969, p. 2). Those within the same social networks often use similar behaviors and vantage points.

Face-to-face communication offers the opportunity for both verbal and non-verbal communication. It is considered a rich content channel that spreads information through time tested historical methods. The advent of online communication affords greater variety of information management that previous methods need physical interaction to accomplish.

Despite its breadth, online communication channels are less value laden than face-to-face communication. Yet this communication channel is being hedged to create greater reach than would be possible with traditional methods. Varying degrees of information can be collected from networks in the online world that moves quickly among members. Over time, online channels will become more information laden to mimic face-to-face interaction (i.e. video, music, forums).

The authors found that the use of online and off-line communication does have an impact on job performance. The belief is that information is power and the more one is able to collect and integrate varying channels of information the more likely they can make proper decisions that impact their job. It is recommended that business leaders use both forms of communication for maximum job growth.

The report doesn't move into this concept, but through channel expansion theory and concepts of information hubs it is possible to put oneself in the center of the information hub and expand upon that information for greater influence. Leaders who desire to become influential should develop as many communication channels as effectively possible and use that information to bring great ideas forward.

Virtual Communication Creates Online Bonding

Group attachment is an important aspect of retaining and maintaining customers. As groups begin to identify and interact with new members, they build additional identities associated with services and products. Research by Yuquing Ren, et. al (2012), focuses on communication and the understanding of identity, bond, and community identity in online forums. Their study helps highlight how different types of attachment strengthen online interaction and customer retention.

The far majority of business that seeks to build online communities fail to attract a critical mass of customers even when over a million dollars have been spent (Worthen, 2008). The primary problem is that they have not been able to create and develop attachment to their offerings. Customers may have low levels of connection to their offerings and move on after a quick view.

Understanding that there is identity attachment, bond attachment and community attachment to products and services can help in fostering the right type of activities that create positive identity with a company's offerings. Customers should be able to find their personal identities in the product offerings and confirm these findings with a social group.

Identity attachment can be seen as attachment to members who are similar in appearance or other difference that separates them. It is a primarily visual and surface type identity. Bond based attachments are focused more on connection to group members and seeing similarity in belief, interests or values. Group based attachment is focused on connecting to an entire community of online users.

The researchers found that identity based attachment is much easier to foster in online communities. One generally must provide an identity, familiarity of products, and in and out-group type dynamics to encourage retention (i.e. you're different because you use our service). Bond based and community based attachment requires the ability to have personal communications. This is much more akin to social networking than it is other types of online communities.

Online communities act in the same manner as real life communities. Communication is the key component that allows people to feel connected to others and form an identity around particular aspects of interest. In the online world, identity and community groups are easier to establish based upon the specific and general interest in products. Social bonding is more difficult and often takes considerable amount of time and energy. It is difficult to determine precisely when and how long bond identity can be formed. However, the use of profiles and communication around topics can encourage this knowledge of other members.

Using Communication in Difficult Conversations

Serious conversations within the workplace can be difficult for even the most seasoned managers. Managers are often at a crossroads when trying to determine whether to avoid or initiate conversations of destructive employee behavior. Jacquelyn Polito discusses four related approaches that may help managers break through those difficult barriers while still addressing the essential issues (2013). As with all highly emotional discussions, there are a number of considerations to think about before moving forward.

Stone's Five Steps to Productive Conversation (Stone, Patton, & Heen, 2010):

1. Understand the three points of view that are going to be seen within the conversation.

    -Get the facts and be open to new facts.

    -Understand your emotions with the issues.

    -Understand what is at stake.

2. Ensure that the conversation is worth having and if it is the best approach.

3. Explain the story from a third party's point of view to reduce conflict.

4. Explore both your and their sides of the story.

5. Problem solve to rectify the situation.

Leebov's Caring Feedback Model (Leebov 2010): To provide caring feedback without stepping down.

1. State your purpose in positive terms.

2. State the situation and behavior in clear terms.

3. State the consequences on others when such behavior continues.

4. Use empathy.

5. Make it a dialogue, allow for responses, and ask questions.

6. State your request and expectations in clear terms.

Ury's Break through Strategies (Ury 1993): A model to break through the barriers to resolution that include emotions, power, position, dissatisfaction and reaction.

1. Imagine you are looking down on your conversation and avoid reaction or giving in.

2. They may show anger, hostility, resentment, or aggressiveness. Avoid engaging in argument in the way they expect and continue to work on problem solving.

3. Don't reject their position only reframe it.

4. If the employee does not want to see the mutual benefits don't push but simply explain how it benefits all parties.

5. Educate them on the futile nature of not working with others and achieving mutual goals.

Crawford's Workplace Issue Discussion (Crawford 2008): The manager should assume the leadership role, be calm, and directly address the behavior while being concise.

1. Describe the purpose of the meeting.

2. Describe the behavior.

3. Listen to the reaction.

4. Agree on the resolution and set expectations.

5. Hear employees side of story.

6. Work on problem-solving and collaboration.

7. Document discussion.

8. Reinforce.

Supportive and Humanistic Leaders are More Effective

Both style and communication intertwine tightly around the effectiveness of leaders. Reinout de Vries and Angelique Bakker-Pieper conducted research on 279 employees in government agencies to understand the communication styles on human-oriented and leadership outcomes (2010). They used the six main communication styles of verbal aggressiveness, expressiveness, preciseness and assuredness, supportiveness and argumentativeness.

Leadership communication style bases its effectiveness on the need to maximize hierarchical relationships to reach goals (Daft, 2003). Communication has a purpose and is goal oriented. Communication seeks to enhance and influence the environment in one form or another. The ultimate goal is often dependent on the leader who seeks either collective or self-gain.

Communication is about knowledge sharing. It is a process where individuals exchange tacit and explicit information to create new knowledge (Van den Hoof and De Ridder, 2004). Communication helps participants bring forward new information and connect them together in ways that have more meaning for them. The more someone communicates with others the more they understand both the issues at hand and the potential solutions.

Charismatic and human-oriented leadership correlated with perceived leadership performance, satisfaction with that leader, and employee's commitment. Likewise, Leadership supportiveness had a strong correlation with knowledge sharing. Both styles were stronger than correlations with task-oriented leadership.

The authors contend that leadership supportiveness appears to be the strongest communication approach and has positive associations with leadership styles and outcome. This find makes sense if we consider that leadership is about influence and drawing people in through supportive, humanistic, and knowledge sharing behaviors that helps others solve their own problems and sets higher expectations. Leaders who excessively focus on tasks may be less successful if their subordinates do not understand the greater purpose of the tasks, do not feel connected to it, and do not know how to achieve it.

Communication Builds Higher Cognitive Models

Workplace communication and cross-culture interaction can help foster greater levels of collaborative effort. A paper by Huber & Lews (2011) highlights how heuristics and bias are a platform for first understanding others but additional information creates stronger cognitive models. It is these models within groups or across groups that adjust overtime to create mutual development.

When individuals understand each other's cognitive models they create cross-understanding (Huber & Lewis, 2010). Cross-understanding can also occur on a group level whereby a cognitive model for a group and their vantage point has been developed. Knowing how your communication partners think and understand can be beneficial for relating information in a way in which it is palatable and creating shared understandings.

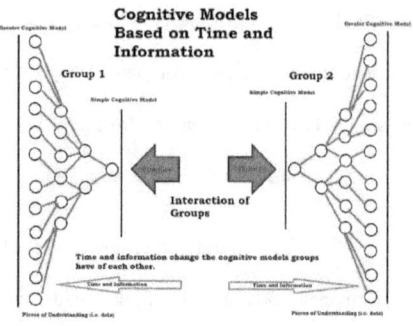

Shared understandings range from low to high in terms of their accuracy and quantity of information. Some may know very little about other groups while some may have a great deal of experience. This is a level of shared social theory or shared social understanding. This is generally based in familiarity, cross-communication, and reflection. Even members within the same group may have different understandings of others even though they have shared traits.

People come to understand each other through default templates that are full of assumptions. As they interact with others, communicate, share experiences, and see how others act in certain situations they come to update those templates. It is a process of offering new information based within real life experience.

Conflict is often caused by misunderstandings or unreasonable behavior. The more groups interact and share relevant information the better the decisions of the group. This process can only work if members are free to talk, share ideas, and brainstorm the possibilities. Group think occurs when individuals are not free to communicate leading to one sided vantage points and strategies.

Over compliance to group norms, assumptions and rules creates 1.) a lack of new information, and 2.) poorer overall decisions that limit cross understanding. Group assumptions based on heuristics create faster reactions but also limit the potential to be accurate in decision-making. Quick assumptions are regularly faulty as they are confined by a lack of available information.

The paper brings forward concepts that may be useful to businesses that are either in the process of developing stronger teams or would like to reduce encampment within their ranks. People often choose to work with others that are similar to themselves. Each brings forward their own cognitive model based with quick heuristic platforms. As they interact with each other it broadens their ability to understand the other. When these cognitive platforms are different than other members of the same group there is pressure overtime to solidify them into shared conscious understandings (i.e. the stream of conscious).

Communication as Strategy Projection

Strategy is not only the logical components of actions that lead to goal achievement. True strategy has significant social aspects based within the cognitive understanding of workers, stakeholders, and even customers. A paper by Vallaster and Muehlbacher (2012) outlines the social representations inherent within strategy formation and its social context of development.

Strategic success must take into account actions, interactions, and negotiations of multiple actors. Each person realizes the strategy through his or her own vantage points and previous practices. Strategy must fit within others mental framework in order to be successful and fully implemented throughout an organization.

Strategizing takes includes 1.) narratives, 2.) actors personal interests, 3.) organizational design, culture and past practices, and 4.) market factors. Strategic development should take into account the multiple factors and their potential weight in order to be successful and navigate the social environment.

Individual context-dependent interpretations influence the way in which people make decisions. As new information is presented it changes past schemata to that which is in transition and finally to new schemata. Thus, each strategy is situation dependent on the understandings of those involved in its formation and those who are going to carry it out. It naturally changes the way they think about such strategies.

Strategy is also dependent on the internal workings and actors of an organization. Through the process of strategic development a company's practices and cultural perceptions will affect a strategies fulfillment. In other words, the way in which people think will influence how they see the strategy and its potential benefits for themselves. It is this self-interest that eventually produces "buy in".

As most strategies seek to find competitive advantages, the market and various outside stakeholders will create pressure on the strategy and influence its perception. As the human mind considers the effectiveness of potential strategies these external factors, will act in judgment and will naturally create pressures. Poor strategy that does not consider the external structure and pressures is likely to fail.

The way in which society views itself and interacts with itself will influence strategy through social representations. Social representations are 1.) complex formations of knowledge that comes from social discourse, and 2.) socio-cognitive processes that come from that discourse. As something new enters into society's awareness there is a communication process that comes to define it. In other words, society settles on meaning.

Strategies consist of core and peripheral elements. Core strategies are seen as logical and have shared cognitions based within the common perspectives of the participants (i.e. customer oriented service as a strategy). According to the authors, the actor must believe in their realities and put those forward to others but should be willing to bend these understandings to create shared realities among a group of people. This produces higher levels of agreement.

Each person within the strategic structure will have to make personal meaning from it. Therefore, each participant has sub-strategies related to their place within the strategy based within their memories and understandings (Barsalou, 1999). They use their past experiences to find meaning within the strategy and build personal sub-strategies from it.

The peripheral aspects of the strategies include those who are not directly related to the strategy formation but may be impacted by it. For example, customers who have needs of quality and experience should have their information considered as this improves upon the strategies effectiveness. Without understanding the impact on the environment or others, it is doubtful such strategies will be fully effective. Ineffective strategies can lead to lower profits and lost marketplace.

The authors bring forward the concept that the context strategy formation is as much social as it is logical. Logic is the center but its social aspects are the periphery. All strategic decisions must take into account the impact and perceptions of others. When stakeholders cannot make meaning or formulate a social connection to the strategy, it is unlikely to be fruitful. Without some type of personal cognitive agreement people will reject the strategy and the company's offerings.

The authors dance around the concept of social projection. Projection is a concept brought forward by Freud to describe how one unconsciously projects their traits onto another. Social projection in strategy is the idea that strategy is built from the inner and outer understandings of the maker(s) and can be projected forth into and from a group. For example, a company that is losing their financial and competitive position may rally their executives to formulate a strategy. Once that strategy has been created, it can be projected onto others within the organization in the attempt to foster actions that fulfill the goals of that strategy. Social projection can lead to social behavior based upon varying factors inherent in the environment that lead to agreement or rejection.

Communication Networks within the Workplace

Communication is social by nature, helps others to engage in relationships, and link the micro actions of individuals to the macro actions of the organization. The communication patterns of a workplace determine not only the culture and flavor of the company but also its effectiveness. The researchers Keyton, et. al. (2013), discuss the nature of communication in the workplace and the patterns formed.

Employees who are effective communicators are likely to succeed in achieving their goals. Individuals are seen as active agents whose behaviors are driven by motivations that are innate (Bandura, 2008). Such individuals express themselves, their personalities, and even their unconscious conflicts through communication.

Let us take two examples of people who have distinct communication patterns within the workplace. Tom wants to be successful and seeks recognition for his work. John feels as though he is more deserving of others and the only way to achieve his goals is to dominate others around him. Both will develop a communication pattern to meet their goals.

Tom talks about the great things he has done and seeks recognition and approval. John is hyper critical and talks poorly of others abilities. Tom likes to talk out differences while John seems to push his agenda on others. Tom learns from others and John negatively compares himself to others. Both have developed a pattern.

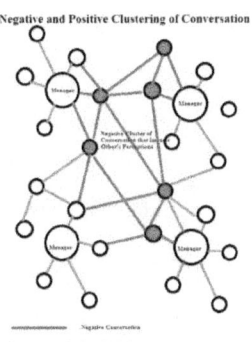

Negative and Positive Clustering of Conversation

Tom and John's behaviors are likewise both addictive. Communication is social and others gauge their environment by the behaviors around them. If Tom works hard, manages conflict, and seeks recognition and this results in success others will begin to copy Tom. If John's brashness and negativity is rewarded others will assume his process fosters success. One workplace will become more productive while the other will become more toxic.

Of course, Tom and John are not the only people in the workplace. Therefore, the total communication flow is based upon up the collective pattern of the environment. These patterns are defined as the culture and value systems of a company. To change culture and patterns means to change the conversations, reward systems, and basic economic assumptions of the environment.

The researchers sought to understand what communicative behaviors the workplace has experienced based upon the perception of employees. Within their target they found that the ten most common verbal communication patters were listening, asking questions, discussing, sharing information, agreeing, suggesting, getting feedback, seeking feedback, answering questions and explaining. These observed patterns suggest a workplace that seeks to be efficient and the communicative patterns appear to support that effort.

A second study found some differences. Routinely used verbal communication behaviors exhibited were information sharing, relational maintenance, expressing negative emotion, and organizing. Even though each of these are common, it should be understood that relational maintenance should not be excessive and expressing negative emotion should be productive. If they do not add to the success of the organization, it is possible that excessive amounts of time in social structure maintenance and negativity can create a non-mobile and toxic workplace.

Understanding what communication patterns employees are using can determine overall cultural values and communicative behaviors within the workplace. Surveying employee's perceptions of communication patterns within the workplace will help solidify for decision-makers the most common interactions. By understanding these patterns, it is possible to make adjustments that further help the organization develop proper workplace assumptions that lead to productivity.

When conducting similar studies it may be beneficial to break up the surveys into the following:

1.) Executive Communication Patterns: How do executives communicate with each other and employees?

2.) Employee Communication Patterns: How do employees perceive the communication patterns within the workplace?

3.) Employee to Customer Communication Patterns: How do customers perceive the communication patterns emulating from employees?

Communication Impacts Perceptions of Power

Most people who have been in the working world for some time have come across a situation where a single person uses power and authority with a dominating communication style to push their will on a corporate board, team, or workplace. Research by Tost, et. al (2013) discusses some of the pitfalls of doing so and the eventual decline of team performance. As performance declines so does the ability of organizations to generate income through collaborative effort and idea generation.

Politicized workplaces are stressful and generally unproductive. According to Eisenhardt and Bourgeois (1988), when there is power inequality within the workplace political conflict rises and team performance declines. Teams should be well balanced to ensure that there is equity of power and the ability to discuss concepts openly for better idea generation.

Power should be used to help push good ideas through to create greater productivity. However, when power is used to diminish the brainstorming process the best ideas do not come forward. There is a natural propensity for people to defer all major decisions to those that have the formal power. We all know that those that have the formal power do not always know the right answers or have failed to grasp alternative positions. Power, Leadership and Formal Authority can be summed up as follows:

Power: The ability of a person to control outcomes, how people perceive expenses, or push people in certain behaviors (Keltner, et. al, 2003).

Leadership: The ability to influence others to work toward group objectives and goals (Bass, 2008).

Formal Authority: Holding a position that that allows for a specific role within social hierarchy (Peabody, 1962).

Power, leadership, and formal authority maintain the ability to influence the outcomes of the group's decisions. There are times when this can be beneficial once a final decision has been made and concise action is needed. However, preempting or cutting short the decision process may end up costing the organization later in terms of strategic outcomes as well as future willingness of employees to express themselves fully.

Open communication within teams is essential in determining of the team's performance (Dionne et. al, 2004). Common knowledge would indicate that the more freethinking employees are the more likely better decisions are made. Strategic decision making requires the ability to perceive and understand the various outcomes. As thoughts build on each other, open communication affords a better brain storming session.

The authors conclude that the formalization of power into the hand of an individual limits the overall team performance. The leader's subjective perspectives of power lead them to seek additional power derailing the performance process. The more power a leader feels the more their behavior changes and the more people defer to their power. Followers must willingly give up the power for the leader to gain additional influence.

The research is important for avoiding the concepts of "group think" which limits a team's performance. As leaders become more engrained in the perception of their power gain, the more their behavior prompts team members to give up the authority. The end result of such power deference is poor decisions, poor consequences, and potentially disastrous results. Even though it is possible for a single person to break the cycle by asking the right questions the social structure may try and force adherence leading to a lack of empowerment and performance for the whole group.

Conclusion

Communication is based within the human species and is integrally tied to our intimate nature. The verbal and non-verbal patterns are defined by our biological development. This breaks communication into honest and dishonest forms. Honest communication is that which connects all of the aspects of language with body and fits within the context of the environment.

People know when language is disingenuous on a subconscious level but may never become aware of the meaning behind language unless they have developed intra-intelligence.

All communication is goal oriented and based within the personality of the person. Recurring themes, patterns, and word choices help define the needs of the person and what they are seeking from the environment. This is difficult for many to understand as it requires understanding of a person in various places, times and events to regress back to the root of their messages. To understand other people is to know what motivates them and this can be a powerful tool in business.

All language is about sharing cognitive models and the way in which individuals see the world. The more people communicate the more likely they are to understand each other's needs. All knowledge is a social construction process where each person builds higher or lower cognitive models based upon the environment in which they live and the cues they are receiving from that environment.

Conflict is a result of two different cognitive models clashing for influence. These models are often based upon the social group in which one exists. Language is a cultural phenomenon that is embedded within their reality construction. Groups and beliefs can be defined by the language and perceptions individuals use. To bring people together requires the development of shared cognitive models focused around a goal or objective both parties can agree with. Even though they use different processes and strategies to get there the agreement of a basic goal helps them formalize a direction.

Coming to an understanding is not easy as individual cognitive models impact what they see in the environment. Someone may literally be blind to another's vantage point until they have incorporated a way of understanding the concepts in their own mind. Selective attention focuses on that information which fits within their mental perspectives and ignores other information that is considered repugnant. To get someone to see your vantage point requires densely knit information that bridges from their-to-your perspective.

It is sometimes not possible to do this directly as people regularly reject arguments that counter their perceived goals and beliefs. To break through their resistance requires the transference of information in piece-meal pattern that does not directly attack their core beliefs and identities. When the information has been transferred and incorporated sufficiently it is possible to create the bridging piece that allows them to connect the information into a new perspective. Effectiveness in influence requires a rerouting of their goals into more productive win-win situations.

It is possible to also see this as mini agreements that lead up to a larger agreement. A person who is resistant to certain ideas may be more willing to accept non-threatening information and come to an agreement with that information. Once enough information has been incorporated into their cognitive model that model begins to change. New information produces shifts in the model and how justifications of "ifs" and "thens" are formalized.

As language is group phenomenon, the word choices of the leaders and the patterns within organization will define not only the culture of that organization but also group's behavior. A single organization may have more than one group and their cognitive models are easily discernable if you look for the honest language they project. Cohesive organizations used similar language with individual expression based within a person's background and environmental influences.

Communication takes many forms in today's world. Even though it is rooted in our biology it can be projected through both face-to-face and virtual methods. Modern technology has afforded the opportunity to mimic true language through higher levels of content. Face-to-face language offers a richer channel of content but virtual communication has a longer reach and can be used to spread messages to the farthest corners of the earth. As technology becomes faster, the ability to spread language and higher cognitive models becomes more likely.

Leaders who seek to be influential must learn to master their face-to-face communication, virtual projections, and their ability to raise others cognitive models. To influence a group means that one must understand the current cognitive models they are using and add to that model to create higher levels of understanding that motivates actions. Effective leaders can use their charisma matched with the multiple communication channels to create shared understandings that draw adherents around particular causes.

References

Bandura, A. (2008). Social cognitive theory. In W. Donsbach (Ed.),

Barsalou, L. W. (1999): Perceptional Symbol Systems. *Behavioral and Brain Science, 22* (1999).

Bass, B. M. 2008. *The Bass handbook of leadership: Theory, research, and managerial applications.* New York: Free Press.

Beatty, M. J. & McCroskey, J. C. (1998). Interpersonal communication as temperamental expression: A communibiological paradigm. In J. C. McCroskey, J. A. Daly, M. A. Martin, & M.

J. Beatty (Eds.), *Communication and personality: Trait perspectives* (pp. 41_67). Cresskill, NJ: Hampton.

Bidelman, et. al. (2013). Tone language speakers and musicians share enhanced perception and cognitive abilities for musical pitch: evidence for bidirectionality between the domains of language and music. *PlosOne, 8*(4).

Burgoon, J. & Hale, J. L. (1987). Validation and measurement of the fundamental themes of relational communication. *Communication Monographs, 54,* 19_41.

Choi, S. & Hattrup, K. (2012). Relative contribution of perception/cognition and language on spatial categorization. *Cognitive Science, 36* (1).

Crawford D. (2008). *We need to talk: ten scenarios to practice handling needed conversations. Society for Human Resource Management.* SHRM. Retrieved October 7th, 2013 at http://www.shrm.org/education/hreducation/documents/we%20need%20to%20talk.pdf

Daft, R. (2003). *Management (6th Edition).* Cincinnati, Oh: South-West.

Dennis, et. al. (2008). Media, tasks, and communication processes: a theory of media synchronicity. *MIS Quarterly, 32* (3).

De Vries & Bakker-Pieper, W. (2010). Leadership=communication? The relations of leaders' communication styles with leadership styles, knowledge sharing and leadership outcomes. *Journal of Business & Psychology, 25* (3).

Dionne, et. al (2004). Transformational leadership and team performance. *Journal of Organizational Management, 17*: 177–194.

Eisenhardt, K. & Bourgeois, L. (1988). Strategic decision making in high-velocity environments: Toward a midrange theory. *Academy of Management Journal, 31*: 737–770.

Gitomer, J. (2013). Presentation and communication skills. *Corridor Business Journal, 9* (35).

Huber, G. & Lewis, K. (2011). Cross-understanding and shared social theories. *Academy of Management Review, 36* (2).

Huber, G. P., & Lewis, K. (2010). Cross-understanding: Implications for group cognition and performance. *Academy of Management Review, 35*: 6–26.

Johns, W. & Young, N. (2012). Power of persuasion: becoming the influencer. *Facilities Manager, 28* (3)

Keltner, et. al. (2003). Power, approach, and inhibition. *Psychological Review,* 110: 265–284.

Keyton, J. et. al. (2013). Investigating verbal workplace communication behaviors. *Journal of Business Communication, 50* (2).

Leebov W. (2010). *Elevating performance: how to raise the bar.* Wendy Leebov, Inc. Retrieved October 7th, 2013 at http://www.quality-patient-experience.com.

Mishra, B. (2009). Role of paralanguage in effective English communication. *The Icfai University Press*; India

Markus, H. R. & Kitayama, S. (1991). Culture and the self: Implications for cognition, emotion, and motivation. *Psychological Review, 98,* 224_253.

Mitchell, J. (1969). "The concept and use of social networks" in social networks in urban situations, J.C. Mitchell (ed), Manchester, England: Manchester University Press, p. 1-50.

Morton & Trehub, S. (2001). Children's understanding of emotion in speech. *Child Development, 72* (3).

Md Zani, et. al. (2011). The relationship between lecturers' paralanguage and student's satisfaction in Universiti Teknologi Mara, Kendah, Malaysia. *Interdisciplinary Journal of Contemporary Research in business, 3* (6).

McCrae, R. R. & Costa, P. T. (1996). Toward a new generation of personality theories: Theoretical contexts for the Five-Factor Model. In J. S. Wiggins (Ed.), *The Five Factor Model of Personality: Theoretical perspectives* (pp. 51_87). New York, NY: Guilford Press.

Norton, R. (1978). Foundation of a communicator style construct. *Human Communication Research, 4,* 99_112.

Peabody, R. (1962). Perceptions of organizational authority: A comparative analysis. *Administrative Science Quarterly,* 6: 463–482.

Polito, J. (2013). Effective communication during difficult conversations. *Neurodiagnostic Journal, 53* (2).

Schramm, W. (Ed.). (1954). *The process and effects of mass communication.* Urbana, IL: University of Illinois Press.

Stone, D., Patton, B., and Heen, P. (2010). *Difficult Conversations: How to Discuss What Matters Most.* New York: Penguin Books.

The international encyclopedia of communication[electronic version]. London, England: Blackwell. doi:10.1111/ b.9781405131995.2008.

Tost, et. al. (2013). When power makes others speechless: the negative impact of leader power on team performance. *Academy of Management Journal, 56* (5).

Ury W. (1993). *Getting Past No: Negotiating Your Way from Confrontation to Cooperation.* New York: Bantam Books.

Van den Hoof & Hendrix, (2004*). Eagerness and willingness to hare: the relevance of different attitudes towards knowledge sharing.* Paper presented at the Fifth European Conference on Organizational Knowledge, Learning and Capabilities: Innsbruck, Australia.

Vallaster, C. and Muehlbacher, H. (2012). Strategy formation as social representation: understanding the influence of contexts on strategy formation. *Betriebswirtschaft/Business Administration Review, 72* (5).

Waldherr, A. & Muck, P. (2011). Towards an integrative approach to communication styles: the interpersonal circumplex and the five-factor theory of personality as frames of reference. *Communications: The European Journal of Communication Research, 36* (1).

Walchli & Cysouw, M. (2012). Lexical typology through similarity semantics: toward a semantic map of motion verbs. *Linguistics, 50* (3).

Wang, D. & Li, H. (2007). Nonverbal language in cross-cultural communication. *US-China Foreign Language, 5* (10).

Worthen, B. (July 16,2008). *Why most online communities fail.* Wall Street Journal.

Yuqing Ren, et. al. (2012). Building member attachment in online communities: applying theories of group identity and interpersonal bonds. *MIS Quarterly, 36* (3).

Zhang, Y. (2013). The politeness principles in business negotiation. *Cross-cultural communication, 9* (4).

Zhang, X. & Venkatesh, V. (2013). Explaining employee job performance: the role of online and offline workplace communication networks. *MIS Quarterly, 37* (3).

Putting it Together

A leader is one who knows the way, goes the way, and shows the way.-John C. Maxwell

Putting it All Together

Successful transformation of organizations rest on strategy, leadership, path-goal, and communication. Knowing when to change and why to change is an important part of building stronger companies. This is one of the most difficult aspects of leadership. Few see the need for change and even fewer have a desire to go through the stress of enacting reform. This inability to predict trends and put forward adequate effort may be one of the pivotal reasons why companies decline. It is like pushing a locomotive down the same track at ever faster speeds even though that track leads to the wrong destination. Successful leaders should predict where they are going and understand even more complex information than in the past to make accurate decisions to see the need for change.

Strategy and Path-Goal

Executives who seek to stay on top of the market should develop the ability to analyze a wide array of information in order to effectively predict markets. They use available market information, company research, and rely on their experience to make decisions. It is the ability to formalize information into a cohesive framework to understand changes as they occur. Strategy formation requires moving ambiguous information to something more concrete for testing and implementation.

Moving something from its hazy existence to a clear strategy takes time and research. This period of exploration delves into meeting knowledgeable persons, open conversations, data collection, analysis of alternatives and finding expertise. As each path and decision has many other possible outcomes, based on internal and external pressures, inherent within those situations it is not easy to set upon a course with unverified haste.

Decisiveness is welcome but unyielding ignorance should be avoided. Collecting the right information that allows one to make an educated decision backed by research is better than snap judgments rooted in anecdotal evidence. When strategies are enacted that are not aligned with the market the outcome can be disastrous. As money and resources are funneled into poor strategies they will continue to eat additional resources.

Effective strategies may take considerable resources and time to achieve goals but are more effective than poor strategies. Incorrectly aligned strategies will consume excessive resources that it cannot return from the market. This is the natural effectiveness of on target thinking versus hazy judgments that are not based within the market. Focusing on understanding the market and then making strategic judgments is more effective than making judgments based upon limited personal experience alone.

As an organization aligns its efforts and resources it creates a natural trajectory that will impact its future. If that trajectory is accurate the company will receive financial rewards through increased sales and market share. If those efforts are misaligned the organization will waste time and resources on the wrong path. At some point an organization may go through a critical threshold where recovering from an improper path is no longer possible. The time, money, effort, and resources are not enough to correct the situation and the organization will be sold or move into bankruptcy.

Think of strategy like a space shuttle launching into some far reaching place in space. An abundance of background information is needed before charting a course. If there is a major miscalculation there is no way the shuttle will have the fuel to correct its improper trajectory. However, if that shuttle discovers the error right after launch it can continually adjust its trajectory to hit the right target. Before a strategy will even remotely be successful it must be shooting into the right quadrant. Executives should not have blindfolds on when launching their projects into the market. They should be focusing their efforts on researching and understanding the market and the internal resources of the organization to make educated decisions.

The path is created by the market but a strategy will determine which path is most appropriate. Effective strategies will use mental resources to find the right path. The path is the process of organizational alignment that focuses closely on market needs. Experience, research, and intelligence are used to determine which paths are likely to achieve desired outcomes.

Leadership and Communication

The development of a strategy and the formation of a path are not enough. People must know about this strategy if they are expected to follow it and create organizational alignment. The right leader with proper characteristics can project this strategy and create motivation in employees on a deeper cognitive level. They are able to relay the information in a way that makes it believable and beneficial to others. The right leadership, in the right environment, and at the right time will make all of the difference in focusing organizational effort.

The strategy and formation of the path allow for clarity in communication. Knowing where the organization wants to go, how it is going to get there, and the resources the organization has to achieve its goals exudes confidence. People become distinctly aware that the leader has thought through all of the alternatives and their judgment can be trusted with employee effort.

This process is furthered by sharing cognitive models. When employees ask questions and reasonable answers they begin to trust leaders. If these answers skirt around essential issues or appear to be holding back information that impacts them they will naturally not trust the message or the messenger. Their cognitive model will focus more on their own interests than the collective interest.

Cognitive models adjust and change only through communication and information. Those who do not communicate well are not able to influence others at a significant level to spark change. It is important to engage in communication, share information, receive feedback and provide responses. An open process of communication encourages trust.

This trust is based in the perception of the truthfulness of the leader. If that leader has built a reputation of lying or misrepresenting the truth through inaccurate statements and comments, it can damage credibility. A lack of credibility means that followers will second guess their messages and seek alternative information before trusting the speaker. This slows down the change process as well as the willingness of people to engage in that change.

As each person hears the message they will transform it and spread it to the next person depending on their personal needs. The personality of the leader and their goals has a lot to do with how this message is interpreted or spread to others. When a positive message turns negative it is because of the perceptions of the person interpreting, using it, and transforming it have adjusted the message.

Body language and context has as much to do with how we are viewed by others as the words that we use. People naturally watch the entire person, their demeanor, tone, and pace of speech to determine hidden meaning within the messages. This doesn't mean they are actively seeking this meaning but subconsciously retaining useful data for their own biological survival. This is one reason why someone will say they trust or don't trust a person and develop a perception that is difficult to solidify in specifics or facts.

The very way in which a person is perceived will enhance or taint their message. Each word is sifted through the listener's mental filters and adjusted based upon their perspective. For example, a person who doesn't trust a particular leader will hear more disconfirming messages through selective attention when compared to positive messages. It will take time, transparency, and consistency of message to overcome negative filters. This change would mean the listener is open to alternative information.

Having different methods of communicating at varying times is also important. People move through biological rhythms and daily life distractions that may impact what they hear and how they interpret it. Stating a consistent root message in multiple forms and multiple ways helps in ensure that they are receiving the message at a time that is palatable to them. The more often they hear the message in varying forms the more likely they will be open to receiving and processing it. In other words, it will make it past their mental filters.

It is possible to use face-to-face, company literature, announcements, social media, and videos to create this consistent theme. The more consistent the fundamental principles of the message the more likely people will be able to view that message as consistent and trustworthy. They will take a piece from one communication channel and add it to other pieces from other communication channels to create the totality of message and their perception of it.

As technology advances leaders will find they have influence that reaches beyond their organizations and into the wider world. With lightning speed videos, posts, and articles are available for the whole world to ponder. No longer are leaders' influencers only within the organization but also part of national and international dialogue about interesting topics and policies. People will rely more closely on their information to make meaning out of their environment and determine what actions are most beneficial to them.

The Strategy, The Path, The Leader and Communication

Once the strategy is developed the path is set upon. This may be a long or short-term path depending on the objectives and resources of the company. The Leader communicates what must be accomplished to stay on that path and helps other's envision the possibilities. When followers begin to align their efforts the organization begins to transform. It is this transformation process that allows companies to maintain long-term sustainability in an ever adjusting market. Each path leads to different opportunities and failures. The organizational members are the ones who must be willing to walk the path while the leader tells them which path and where that path leads. Each step gets the group closer to the final goal and to achieving new heights. The willingness to follow is an important reflection of the leader's capacities and communication style in encouraging employees to act.

The leader has the responsibility to draw the cognitive model to a point of focus so that those with personal and organizational resources will align with defined objectives. When communication provides mixed signals or unclear objectives it is not fair to expect followers to intuitively make meaning out of these messages and know which course is best for them. The bridging of the mental and physical divide happens when new connections are made and new behaviors are exhibited.

Leaders that can step above their limitations will hit transcendence. They watch the patterns within the chaos and encourage the formation of stronger organizations that focus on meeting objectives. They understand the psychological depth by which people make decisions and can see the macro adjustments within the environment. As the each person aligns to the strategy the transcendental leaders can encourage greater connectivity, motivation, and effort to develop a growth engine. These leaders know that the only true motivation is through the individual who must find meaning within their environment to expend their effort on something even beyond the objectives of the organization or the needs of the leaders who guide them. They create an organic system complete with motivations, guidance, social encouragement, and challenge that is self-enhancing and self-sustaining long after the leader is gone.

www.ingramcontent.com/pod-product-compliance
Lightning Source LLC
Chambersburg PA
CBHW051808170526
45167CB00005B/1931